DRIVE SAFELY PUBLISHING

A Complete Guide to Overcoming Driving Anxiety

Practical Strategies for Building Confidence, Staying Calm, and Driving with Ease

Contents

1

Copyright © 2025 by Drive Safely Publishing

All trademarks, service marks, product names, or brand names mentioned in this book are the property of their respective owners and are used only in an educational context. No endorsement by, or affiliation with, those entities is implied.

The guidance provided in this book does not replace official laws, regulations, or professional advice from medical providers, licensing authorities, or certified driving instructors. Always consult qualified professionals when making decisions about health, driving ability, or legal requirements.

2

Disclaimer

This book is intended solely as an educational resource to support drivers in managing and reducing driving anxiety. It is not a substitute for professional medical advice, psychological counseling, legal guidance, or official recommendations from state licensing authorities, law enforcement, or certified driving specialists.

Every driver's situation is unique. Factors such as health conditions, medications, mental health, and personal driving history all influence how anxiety affects driving ability. Readers are strongly encouraged to consult with their healthcare providers, mental health professionals, or other qualified specialists for individualized advice and treatment.

While this guide offers strategies, tools, and exercises to promote confidence and safety, driving always involves risks. Road conditions, weather, traffic, and other unpredictable factors can create situations beyond the scope of this book. Ultimately, each driver is responsible for assessing their readiness, making sound decisions behind the wheel, and complying with all applicable traffic laws and regulations.

The author and publisher disclaim any liability for accidents, injuries, damages, or other consequences that may result from the use or misuse of the information contained in this book.

If you experience persistent or severe anxiety, panic attacks, or other mental health concerns related to driving, please seek help from a licensed mental health professional. If you ever feel unsafe or overwhelmed, prioritize your wellbeing and reach out to a healthcare provider or crisis support service immediately.

3

Introduction

You sit in the driver's seat, keys in hand. The engine is quiet. Your heart is not. It thumps hard, sending waves of worry through your chest. Your palms are damp against the steering wheel. You want to drive. You need to get somewhere. But right now, the idea of moving the car feels bigger than you. You stare out at the road ahead, filled with doubt, frustration, and even shame. Why can't you just drive like everyone else?

If this scene feels familiar, you are not alone. Millions of adults face driving anxiety every day. Some have felt it since their very first lesson. Others found it after a frightening event—a near miss, a panic attack, or a bad memory that won't let go. No matter how it started, driving anxiety can feel like an invisible wall. That wall stands between you and the freedom that driving offers.

Driving is much more than just a way to get from one place to another. It is about choice. It is about being able to visit a friend, take your child to school, or accept a new job across town, in other words independence. It is the ability to shape your day and your life. When anxiety makes driving feel impossible, it can shrink your world. You start to depend on others. You turn down invitations. You plan your days around what you can avoid, not what you want to do. The cost is real, and it is not just about missed appointments or errands—it is about missed moments and missed chances.

Picking up this book is a brave step. It is a sign that you want more from life. It shows that you are willing to face your fears, even if your heart is pounding. Seeking help is not weakness. It is courage. You are choosing hope over helplessness, and that choice matters.

The author is a driving school instructor with more than seventeen years of experience and the owner of a driving school. Over the years, thousands of students—teens, adults, seniors, and individuals from all backgrounds—have come through their program. Many were not only learning the rules of the road but also looking for ways to overcome fear and panic behind the wheel. Through this work, the author has seen the impact of small, steady steps and witnessed anxious drivers transform into confident, calm ones. Their approach is built on real-world experience and practical tools, with the belief that every driver can discover confidence, no matter how anxious they may feel today.

You may think you are alone in this struggle. But you are not. In fact, studies show that up to 1 in 3 adults admit to some level of driving fear. On Amazon, hundreds of reviews mention anxiety as a reason for buying books like this one. The shame and silence around driving anxiety make it seem rare, but it is not. It is common, and it does not mean you are failing. It means you are human.

This book promises to walk with you, step by step, toward a calmer and more confident driving life. You will find stories from others who have faced similar fears. You will learn simple skills you can use right away, like breathing techniques, mental rehearsal, and ways to calm your body before and during a drive. You will discover how to break down big fears into smaller, manageable steps. You will also read about how to handle tough moments—like busy intersections, highways, or unexpected panic.

The chapters in this book are designed to build your skills in a clear, steady way. The first section helps you understand where driving anxiety comes from. The second gives you tools to prepare before you even start the car. Next, you will learn in-car techniques for staying calm. Later chapters help you handle stressful situations and recognize the warning signs that tell you it's time to pause. There are tips for dealing with aggressive drivers and ways to make your car a place of comfort and safety. Finally, you will find ideas for building long-term confidence, seeking extra help if needed, and connecting with others who understand.

What makes this book different is its blend of professional experience, proven methods, and real voices. You will see stories from people who have walked this road before you. You will find tools that come from both science and years of teaching anxious drivers. Each chapter gives you something to try right away, so you move forward—not just read about it.

Progress will not happen overnight. Change takes time. Sometimes it will feel slow. Sometimes you will take two steps forward, then one step back. That is normal. Celebrate the small wins: starting the car, driving around the block, or taking a new route. Each step is proof of your effort and your strength. You do not have to do it all at once. You just have to keep going.

As you turn the page, I invite you to see this book as a caring companion. Let it sit beside you as you face your fears and build your confidence. Let it remind you that freedom is possible. Before you begin, pause and think: What is one thing that driving independence would make possible in your life? Hold that hope close. It will guide you through the pages ahead.

You are here. You are ready. The journey to calm, confident driving starts now.

Chapter 1: Understanding Your Unique Driving Anxiety

When I think about driving anxiety, I remember a student in her mid-thirties sitting in my driving school's parking lot. For fifteen minutes she gripped her keys, too nervous to start the car. "I used to love driving," she said. "Now, even the idea of pulling out scares me." If you relate, know that your experience is valid. Just by opening this book, you're showing courage.

Driving anxiety is different for everyone. Some know the exact moment it started—a car accident, panic attack on the highway, or a health scare at the wheel. For others, fear crept in gradually after years of driving with no issue. This anxiety can affect daily choices—routes, jobs, social invitations—and impacts your life in subtle yet significant ways. Your story matters, and you deserve to explore it without judgment.

Mapping Your Driving Anxiety Story

Let's start by gently reflecting on your history with driving and anxiety. Jot notes as you read or use a notebook for these exercises. Think about your earliest driving memories—both positive and challenging. Was there a time driving felt exciting or easy? When did that change? Was there a specific moment when you noticed fear replacing confidence?

Many students find a driving anxiety timeline helpful. Draw a horizontal line on paper, marking significant events like your first lesson, the first time you felt nervous, accidents, proud driving moments, or times you felt discouraged. For some, a panic attack while merging onto a highway stands out; for others, a close call at an intersection might be the last time they drove. Your timeline is personal—there's no right or wrong way to create it.

Consider this prompt: "Describe the last time you felt truly confident behind the wheel." Maybe it was a peaceful solo drive at sunset or a simple errand run without anxiety. Write as much or as little as you like. The goal is honesty, not perfection.

Seeing how anxiety shifts over time can reveal patterns or key turning points. Many experience increased anxiety after incidents like accidents, medical emergencies, or major life changes—moving to a new city, becoming a parent, etc. Some find that after avoiding highways once, their avoidances slowly grew until their world shrank.

Missing out is often part of the story—passing up a child's game due to anxiety, calling in sick when the drive seems overwhelming. These moments can sting, but they're a part of your experience and not unique to you.

You aren't alone. Here are quick snapshots from others with driving anxiety:

- A new immigrant, overwhelmed by city traffic, relied on public transit rather than her car for months.
- A professional, used to city transit, struggled to drive again after moving to the suburbs—each attempt left him shaky.
- A caregiver with twins panicked at the idea of being responsible for her kids' safety and stuck to local roads.

Identifying your experiences shows your reaction is a natural response to real stress and challenge—not weakness. Your story belongs here.

Driving Anxiety Snapshot Worksheet

Try this exercise: On a blank page, make three lists:

- What are my current feelings about driving?

- What challenges do I face most often?
- What would I like to achieve or change through this book?

This worksheet gives you a baseline—a current snapshot. You can use it to track progress and celebrate each small victory.

With gentle curiosity, watch your story take shape. This process isn't just collecting facts—it's about honoring your experience and recognizing every step you're taking toward understanding yourself and your anxiety.

The Science of Panic: What Happens in Your Brain and Body

Picture yourself sitting in your car as your heart pounds, palms sweat, and a chill creeps up your back. Your chest might tighten or your vision narrow—your body sounds every alarm at once. This is panic: powerful, overwhelming, and involuntary. Such responses aren't chosen but stem from deeply rooted human wiring, a survival system dating back to when fleeing from danger was crucial for life.

Central to this is the fight-or-flight response. This ancient alarm system protects you by releasing adrenaline, speeding up your heart, tightening your muscles, and quickening your breath whenever your brain senses danger—real or imagined. It readies you for action, though it can't distinguish between a genuine threat (a bear) and a modern stressor (merging onto a busy highway). To your brain, both feel equally urgent.

The symptoms you feel—trembling, sweating, dizziness, pounding heart—are clear signs your body believes it faces a crisis. You might worry you're losing control or about to faint, causing your thoughts to spiral. "What if I can't breathe? What if I crash?" Such thoughts intensify the physical sensations, forming a feedback loop that sustains anxiety. Waves of heat or chills, nausea, or feeling detached from yourself are also common. Sometimes you may feel as if you're observing everything from outside your own head.

A helpful analogy is the "false alarm system." Imagine a smoke detector that goes off even when there's no fire—just burnt toast. Your brain's anxiety center, the amygdala, acts similarly when you have driving anxiety. It can trigger full panic responses—even without real danger—because it's overprotective, not because you're actually at risk.

The psychological side of panic is as real as the physical. Anxiety wires your brain to expect more panic, especially when driving. Memories of earlier attacks can be so vivid that just thinking about driving triggers symptoms— a phenomenon known as anticipatory anxiety, or "the fear of fear itself." Worrying about another attack can cause the same cycle of physical symptoms, making it hard to break free. "What if" thinking becomes a trap, each worry feeding your body's sense of threat.

Panic often strikes during specific driving situations. One person described his heart racing near highway entrance ramps, gripping the wheel until his knuckles whitened, fearful of losing control. Another experienced shortness of breath and tingling hands in stop-and-go traffic, anxious about escaping if needed. Even bridges or tunnels can trigger panic—your mind imagines no way out and your body responds with an adrenaline surge.

Symptoms like dizziness or tunnel vision are your body's way of focusing resources for "survival," though you're safe in your car. Chest tightness or a lump in your throat can be alarming, but they're classic anxiety signs—not medical emergencies.

Fact vs. Myth: Panic Attack Symptoms

- Myth: "If my heart races this fast, I'll have a heart attack."Fact: A racing heart during anxiety is just your body pumping blood to muscles, not a heart attack.
- Myth: "Dizziness means I'll faint."Fact: While dizzy feelings can be frightening, fainting from panic attacks is rare—blood pressure usually rises, not falls.
- Myth: "Chest pain or trouble breathing means I'm suffocating."Fact: Chest tightness and breathlessness come from muscle tension and rapid breathing, not actual suffocation.

These sensations are uncomfortable but not dangerous or life-threatening.

Understanding the science won't stop panic instantly, but it helps you see these feelings as false alarms, not warnings of disaster. Your body is using old survival wiring to respond to modern situations. Even when intense, these sensations are temporary and survivable—your system naturally calms down when the threat passes. This knowledge empowers you to face—and eventually quiet—your anxious mind and body on the road.

Pinpointing Your Triggers: Highways, Intersections, and More

When it comes to driving anxiety, triggers are personal. What rattles one person may not faze another, and sometimes, even you're surprised by what sets off your nerves. The first step in regaining confidence is learning to spot exactly what makes you uneasy. This isn't about blaming yourself or overanalyzing every moment. It's about bringing some light to places that have felt shadowy and overwhelming, so you can tackle them with clarity instead of fear. I've seen drivers who felt fine on open roads but froze at the idea of left turns across traffic. Others panicked only when parking garages loomed, their minds racing about tight spaces and impatient drivers behind them. Some dreaded night driving, not just because of the dark, but because everything felt harder to judge—distances, speeds, even other drivers' intentions.

You might notice your anxiety spike at certain places: busy intersections with multiple lanes and impatient honking, freeway on-ramps where the flow of traffic never seems to ease up, or narrow bridges that make you feel boxed in. Sometimes it's not a place but a situation—like merging into fast-moving lanes or being stuck at a red light with cars crowding behind you. Many of my students have described the unique dread of being "trapped," unable to exit or escape, even if nothing dangerous is happening.

Triggers can stack up and make each other worse—a concept I call "layered triggers." Maybe you feel okay on highways during the day but add rain and heavy traffic into the mix, and your anxiety skyrockets. Or perhaps merging is tough on its own, but if it happens at night in a construction zone with confusing signs, the stress multiplies. Recognizing these combinations matters; they may explain why some drives are tougher than others.

Try this: over the next week, jot down notes after each drive—what situations or moments made you tense? Did your shoulders climb up toward your ears? Did your stomach knot? Did your breathing change? These are early signs that a trigger is present. Even subtle changes matter. For example:

Trigger Tracker Log (Sample Entry)

- **Date**: Tuesday afternoon
- **Situation**: Approaching a busy intersection
- **Physical Clues**: Sweaty palms, jaw clenched
- **Emotional Clues**: Irritability, urge to turn around
- **Intensity (1-10)**: 7

Looking for these clues in your body and emotions helps you catch anxiety early—sometimes before it grows into panic. You might notice your mind racing ahead with "what if" scenarios or feeling suddenly disconnected from what's happening around you.

Some people resist making lists like this because they worry it'll make things worse. In my experience, naming triggers gives you power over them. It moves them from vague shadows into clear targets you can face directly—and eventually overcome. Think of this as detective work about yourself. No need to judge or rush; just collect information.

Over time, you may see patterns. Maybe night driving is only tough when roads are unfamiliar, or maybe left turns are hardest during rush hour with lots of impatient drivers behind you. Once you see these trends in black and white, the next steps—building coping strategies for each one—become much more manageable.

Why Avoidance Feels Safe—But Keeps You Stuck

Avoidance can feel like a warm blanket on a cold night. When anxiety spikes, sidestepping what scares you brings sweet relief—at least for a moment. Maybe you only drive with a "safe" passenger, or pick quiet back roads, or stick close to home so there's always an easy escape. The pattern makes perfect sense: your brain wants peace, so it pushes you to steer clear of anything that might trigger panic. At first, this works. That wave of dread fades the instant you decide not to take the highway or hand the keys to someone else. The problem is that this short-term comfort comes with a hidden price. Each time you avoid something tough, your world shrinks just a little more.

The cycle is sneaky but powerful. Imagine it as a loop: anxiety creeps in over a certain route or scenario; you sidestep the situation, feeling safe and calm again. But next time that same challenge pops up, the fear returns even stronger, because your brain has learned that avoidance equals safety. It's not your fault—this is how the mind protects itself from perceived danger. Yet with every avoided drive or detour, confidence erodes, and the list of "off-limits" grows longer.

Diagram: The Avoidance-Anxiety Feedback Loop

1. You anticipate fear about driving in a certain situation (like freeways or crowded intersections).
2. You avoid that situation or delegate driving to someone else.
3. Relief and calm return—but only temporarily.
4. Next time, anxiety about the same trigger increases.
5. The urge to avoid gets stronger, so the cycle repeats.

Real life gets complicated fast when avoidance takes the wheel. Maybe you stop accepting invites to friends' houses because they live across town. You might decline a promising job because it requires a commute you don't feel up to. Some people even consider moving neighborhoods or whole cities just to avoid difficult routes or busy traffic. These choices aren't made lightly; they're guided by an urge to keep anxiety at bay. But over time, the cost mounts: missed opportunities, strained relationships, and a growing sense that life is happening elsewhere.

Take the example of only driving with a "safe" passenger—a spouse, sibling, or friend who helps you feel grounded. This can be a useful step during early practice, but when it becomes a rule, independence fades fast. You plan errands around someone else's schedule. You reject last-minute adventures because your "safe" person isn't free. Slowly, reliance replaces confidence, and self-trust becomes harder to find.

Or think about sticking to back roads and avoiding highways altogether. At first, it seems like a clever solution—why suffer if you can sidestep stress? But soon, simple trips balloon into long detours. You spend extra time, energy, and even money just to avoid discomfort. The world feels smaller; the thought of ever returning to busier roads grows more intimidating.

It's important to be honest about how avoidance shapes your days—not with blame or guilt, but with gentle curiosity. Avoidance is not a personal failing. It's not laziness or weakness; it's a coping mechanism that your nervous system uses to keep you safe from distress. Everyone uses it in some way— whether it's skipping social events when feeling down or putting off tough conversations. In the context of driving anxiety, avoidance is simply your mind's way of saying "not today." The trouble is that while it soothes you now, it steals your confidence for tomorrow.

To get perspective on where avoidance shows up in your life, take a few minutes for honest self-reflection. Try this quiz:

- Which roads or routes do I always skip?
- Are there times of day I refuse to drive (nighttime, rush hour)?
- Do I always need a certain person with me in the car?
- Have I made big decisions (job, housing, social plans) based on avoiding specific drives?
- What daily routines have changed because of my anxiety?
- Do I take longer or indirect routes just to avoid certain places?

You don't need to answer every question at once—this isn't about judgment or keeping score. The goal is simply to notice patterns and acknowledge how avoidance might be quietly guiding your choices. Sometimes just seeing these habits on paper brings a sense of clarity and control.

Overcoming the Shame Spiral: You're Not Alone

So many people who struggle with driving anxiety carry a heavy, silent burden: shame. It's the feeling that you're somehow "less than" because others seem to drive with ease, as if fear behind the wheel is a personal flaw. Shame is sneaky—it whispers that you're the problem, that your anxiety is proof you're not strong enough, or that you're failing at a basic skill everyone else has mastered. The truth is far from that. Shame loves secrecy, but it loses its power when you shine a light on it. Facing this feeling openly is one of the bravest things you can do.

There's a myth floating around that if driving makes you anxious, it means you're weak or broken. This myth grows stronger each time someone jokes about "bad drivers" or acts impatient when you hesitate at a stoplight. Maybe you've heard that voice in your own mind: "Everyone else can do it, why can't I?" These thoughts aren't facts—they're just beliefs fueled by stigma and misunderstanding.

Sidebar: Common Myths About Driving Anxiety

- "It's just nerves—real adults get over it."
- "You must have had a traumatic accident to be this scared."
- "If you can't drive, you're not independent."
- "You should be embarrassed to ask for help with something so basic."

None of these are true. Driving anxiety affects millions, regardless of age, background, or driving history ([source 1]). Some people have never been in a crash; others simply grew up in places where driving wasn't needed. The causes and stories are as varied as the people who live them.

I've met a middle-aged father who never let his teenage kids know that he avoided driving on highways for years. He took the long route to every family event, missing out on shared adventures because he didn't want to admit his fear. Then there was a young professional who always found ways to avoid carpooling or road trips with colleagues, coming up with clever excuses rather than telling anyone she was too anxious to drive. Both felt isolated and ashamed—until they found out how common their struggles really were.

The first step to breaking this shame spiral is talking about it, even if it's just with one trusted person. You don't have to share every detail. A simple script might help:

"I'm working on building confidence with driving. Sometimes, I need to take things slow."

This statement is honest, direct, and doesn't require you to apologize or over-explain. You might be surprised how many people respond with understanding or even share their own stories of struggle—sometimes with driving, sometimes with something else entirely. Vulnerability invites connection. It turns out that most of us are hiding fears of our own.

If you want to prepare for a deeper conversation, here's another option:

"I know driving is stressful for me right now. I'm taking steps to work through it and could use some patience and encouragement."

This opens the door for support, rather than judgment. The more you talk about your anxiety, the lighter it feels. Secrets tend to grow heavier in silence.

Setbacks are a normal part of progress—they're not evidence that you've failed, just proof that you're pushing your limits. Maybe you set out to drive across town and ended up turning back halfway; maybe you felt embarrassed about needing to pull over and catch your breath. These moments sting, but they are not final verdicts on your worth or ability. Growth happens in the trying, not just in the triumphs.

Self-compassion matters more than grit here. Progress looks different for everyone—sometimes it means driving one block farther than last week, sometimes it means simply sitting in the car and breathing through discomfort. Give yourself permission to move at your own pace without comparing your path to anyone else's.

If shame starts whispering again, try repeating this affirmation: "Needing support doesn't mean I'm failing—it means I'm human." This simple reminder cuts through the noise of self-judgment and lets you treat yourself with the same kindness you'd offer a friend.

Driving anxiety thrives in isolation but shrinks when shared. Each time you speak up, let someone in, or simply offer yourself grace on a tough day, shame loses its grip a little more. Progress isn't about perfection; it's about showing up for yourself, again and again, even when it feels hard. The road ahead will have twists and bumps, but you don't have to travel it alone. Your courage got you this far—and that matters more than any myth or moment of doubt ever could.

Chapter 2: Preparing for Progress—Foundations and Mindset Shifts

Debunking "Quick Fix" Myths and Setting Realistic Expectations

If you've ever sat in your car, scrolling through your phone, searching for that one secret trick to erase driving anxiety, you're in good company. The idea of a single solution—a "hack," a pill, or a video promising overnight success—is everywhere. I want to be honest with you from the start: there is no miracle fix. Driving anxiety isn't like a light switch you can flip off. It's more like learning a new language or building your fitness; the progress happens layer by layer, sometimes so gradually you barely notice it until you look back.

Rushing the process can backfire. I've seen people leap onto highways after years of avoidance, only to panic and retreat from driving altogether. Forcing yourself into "all-or-nothing" attempts doesn't erase fear; it strengthens it. Research shows gradual exposure—taking small, manageable steps and letting your body adjust—is far more effective than leaping into the deep end without preparation.

Real progress usually unfolds over weeks or months—not days. Some days will feel like breakthroughs; others may feel stuck or even harder than before.

Think of progress as a winding path, not a straight line. Every short trip, every time you turn the key, counts toward building confidence.

Real Talk Progress Checklist

When frustration builds or doubt creeps in, pause and check in with yourself using this simple worksheet:

- I understand that progress happens gradually.
- I expect some drives will go better than others.
- I know setbacks are part of learning.
- I trust that small wins add up over time.
- I am allowed to repeat steps as many times as I need.
- I remind myself that patience is part of the process.

Print this checklist or keep it on your phone for tough days. Use it as a compass when impatience starts to take over.

I wish there was something quicker or easier to offer you, but real change comes from steady practice and self-kindness—not magic solutions. If you catch yourself hoping for overnight results, remember that this is a long-term investment in yourself. Every honest effort you make is a step toward the independence and freedom you want.

Reframing Setbacks: Turning Stumbles into Stepping Stones

Setbacks hurt—it's natural to feel discouraged after a rough drive or panic episode. The important shift is to view these moments not as proof of failure, but as data: information about what helps or hinders you, and how you might adjust for next time. After a tough moment, note what happened, focusing with curiosity rather than judgment. Identify triggers—was it traffic, speed, weather, or something else? Treat each setback as a guide for your next step.

After a challenging drive, reflect quietly on what you learned about your triggers. Did you notice early warning signs like shallow breathing or sweaty palms? Was a particular route or event stressful, like merging or hearing a honk? Pause and ask yourself: "What can I try differently next time?" Maybe you'll adjust your driving time, bring calming music, or drive with a supportive friend. Every stumble is a lesson—not the end of progress.

A setback log can reveal patterns. For example, a parent noticed she felt most anxious when rushed, so she started leaving earlier—making drives less stressful. Another reader realized his hardest drives occurred when he felt isolated, so he reached out to a local support group and began driving short distances with them. Setbacks don't halt progress—they help you find new ways forward.

Negative self-talk often follows setbacks, but kinder words can shift your mindset. Try: "Setbacks mean I'm challenging myself, not failing," or "That was hard, but now I know my limits. Next time, I'll adjust." Keep these affirmations handy—in your phone or on a sticky note in your car. They aren't just comforting; they're practical tools that help reframe your experience.

The Power of Micro-Achievements: Celebrating Every Win

When you struggle with driving anxiety, it's easy to overlook your progress and focus on what you haven't done or how far you are from your goals. But in my years of teaching and coaching anxious drivers, I know that tiny wins matter more than you think. Micro-achievements—like starting the engine just to listen, or sitting behind the wheel for a few minutes without driving— are foundational building blocks for confidence. To outsiders, these may look trivial. But inside, they're major milestones.

Recognizing small wins is not just about self-congratulation; it's about retraining your mind to notice progress rather than problems. Every time you celebrate even a tiny step, your brain learns that progress is possible, which in turn fuels motivation. Motivation builds like a chain reaction: connecting your efforts to rewards makes your brain crave more progress. Scientifically, this is tied to dopamine—the brain's "feel-good" chemical—released whenever you acknowledge achievement, no matter how minor. That little mental boost creates momentum and makes your next step easier.

You can track and celebrate progress in ways that feel natural to you. If gold-star charts remind you of elementary school, make it your own. Many adults prefer custom badge systems: each milestone—a solo lap around the block, a five-minute night drive, or a left turn at a stressful intersection—gets a symbol or badge. Some print these out or sketch them on sticky notes to display at home, while others keep digital or private logs. Here's a sample progress entry: "Today I drove to the store and parked by myself. Felt nervous but did it." That's all—simple and honest.

If a visual approach motivates you, set up a "win wall." Use your fridge, corkboard, or bedroom door to showcase sticky notes or drawings for each milestone—a car for distance, a star for handling tough moments. Over time, this collection visibly charts your progress. If you prefer digital, start a "celebration folder" on your phone. Take selfies after drives or record quick voice memos about what you accomplished and how it felt. These reminders are powerful on tough days when doubt returns.

Sharing and Recording Wins

It helps to share your wins—even tiny ones—with someone supportive: a friend, family, therapist, or fellow anxious drivers online. Sharing is about reinforcing the importance of what you did, not bragging. If you aren't ready to share with others, keep your celebrations private but intentional. Write down each achievement and how you felt before and after—"Nervous but finished," "Scared but didn't quit." Review these on tough days; they'll remind you of your strength and progress.

The Value of Celebrating Small Steps

If you worry celebrating small steps seems silly, dismiss that thought. Anyone who's faced real fear knows how much every tiny advance matters. These actions aren't trivial—they're marks of real courage and persistent effort. They show forward movement, even if it's slow.

So create a system that works for you: badges, sticky notes, photos, audio logs. Remember, only you decide what counts as a win. With every single micro-achievement, you're not just moving closer to your goal, you're showing yourself that progress is real and worth celebrating every time.

Self-Compassion Scripts: Speaking Kindly to Yourself on Difficult Days

Driving can sometimes feel like a test you didn't prepare for, especially when anxiety appears unexpectedly. Maybe you grip the wheel, heart pounding, and critical thoughts pile up: "Why can't I get over this?" or "Everyone else is fine—what's wrong with me?" This self-talk is more than an annoyance; it directly affects how your body handles stress. Research shows that negative self-talk increases stress hormones, prolongs anxiety, and turns each drive into a struggle. It amps up your anxiety while your confidence fades into the background.

Shifting to self-compassion can turn down that anxiety. This isn't about pretending things are fine or forcing positivity. It's about honestly acknowledging your struggle and treating yourself kindly, just as you would with a friend. When you do this, shame and pressure lessen, creating more room for calm and resilience—even if anxiety is still present.

In anxious moments, it's not always easy to find reassuring words. That's why having simple self-compassion scripts helps. You can recall them at a red light, while parked, or before you head out. Try these fill-in-the-blank options: "It's okay to feel _____. I'm doing something brave by _____." For example: "It's okay to feel nervous. I'm doing something brave by driving today." Or remind yourself: "Progress takes time. I can go at my own pace." Even quietly repeating these can help relax your body and mind.

Keep handy, meaningful affirmations close—on a sticky note in your car, your phone's lock screen, or in a small notebook. Good affirmations are short, believable, and fit your situation, such as: "I am learning, not failing." "Every attempt counts, even if imperfect." "I've managed anxious moments before." "Resting doesn't erase my progress." Adapt or write your own, aiming to gently reinforce patience and kindness, not perfection.

For instance, one reader shared that after pulling over during an anxious drive, she usually berated herself. Instead, she tried, "Stopping right now is what I need. Resting is smart—not weak." She took a break, drank water, listened to music, and resumed driving when ready. Speaking kindly didn't erase her anxiety, but it stopped her from spiraling into shame and made future drives easier to approach after setbacks.

Different situations call for specific self-compassion scripts. For pre-drive anxiety: "Feeling anxious doesn't mean I'm not ready—it means I need extra patience today." After a panic attack: "That was tough, but it doesn't cancel my progress." When you start comparing yourself: "My path is my own. No one else has lived my story." If you need help: "Asking for support is smart—it's not giving up." These gentle reminders reinforce that you deserve self-respect and care, even on the most difficult days.

Consider creating a collection of affirmations for various scenarios—one for before driving, another for anxious moments, and one for finishing a drive. You might record yourself saying them to play back on stressful days, place notes in your car or home, set digital reminders, or keep a list you can quickly access.

Self-compassion is a skill that strengthens with practice. At first, it might feel awkward, especially if you're used to being hard on yourself. But choosing kindness over criticism each time helps build emotional resilience, making challenges easier to face. Anxiety may not vanish overnight, but you're creating conditions for growth—without the burden of shame or self-blame weighing you down.

Building a "Progress, Not Perfection" Mindset

If you have ever sat behind the wheel and told yourself, "I have to get this right," you know how much pressure perfectionism can create. This mindset turns every drive into a test and every small mistake into a disaster. Perfection says you must never stall, never hesitate, never feel nervous. It whispers that any slip means failure. Holding yourself to that impossible standard is exhausting. It also makes anxiety worse, because every outing feels like a tightrope walk—one wrong step, and all your confidence comes crashing down. Instead, imagine driving with the attitude that each outing is simply a chance to practice and learn. A progress-focused mindset invites curiosity and patience. It says, "Every drive is useful, no matter how it goes," and lets you celebrate effort instead of chasing flawlessness.

Rigid expectations often set you up for disappointment. Maybe you planned to drive across town, but a traffic jam or tricky left turn sent your heart racing. The perfectionist voice says, "You failed." But a growth mindset notices what you managed, what you learned, and what you might try differently next time. Progress is about flexibility—adapting to stress, life events, and changing moods. When you're tired, anxious, or distracted by work or family, you can adjust your goals. Instead of pushing through with the same plan every day, ask yourself: "What feels manageable right now?" Maybe today's goal is to start the car and breathe for five minutes. Maybe it's driving one block. Other days, you'll feel ready for more.

Try this exercise to make your goals fit your life: On a piece of paper or in your phone notes, write "What does progress look like for me today?" Be honest with yourself. Your answer might change from day to day or even hour to hour. On busy days, it could be as simple as parking in the driveway or reviewing routes on a map. On calmer days, it might mean driving to a farther store or trying out a new street. Giving yourself permission to scale up or down keeps momentum alive and prevents burnout.

Flexibility also means opening up to experimentation. Sometimes you'll try something new—a different route, driving at a quieter time of day, or listening to calming music—and it won't go as planned. Maybe traffic was heavier than expected, or a detour threw you off course. Instead of getting stuck in disappointment, see these moments as valuable experiments. I once worked with someone who decided to take an unfamiliar path home after weeks of following the same routine. She ended up feeling anxious halfway through and needed to pull over. At first, she saw this as proof she wasn't ready. But after reflecting, she realized she'd managed several new turns and handled unexpected construction before needing a break. That was progress—

a collection of small wins within a tough drive.

Rewarding effort over outcome builds resilience. It teaches your brain that trying is worthwhile, even when things feel shaky or don't go as smoothly as hoped. The more you practice this mindset, the less likely you are to abandon your goals when things get tough. You stop measuring success in perfect trips and start counting all the ways you showed up for yourself.

This approach pays off in the long run. Prioritizing progress over perfection leads to real confidence and growing independence behind the wheel. You become less afraid of mistakes and more willing to keep showing up—no matter how many times anxiety tries to slow you down. Over time, driving becomes less about checking boxes and more about building real skills and trust in yourself.

To help you stay on track, here's a checklist of signs you're focusing on progress:

- You notice and celebrate effort—even when results aren't perfect.
- When goals feel too big, you break them down into smaller tasks.
- You adjust plans based on how you feel, not just what you "should" do.
- Trying new strategies feels rewarding, even if they don't always succeed.
- You reach out for support when stuck instead of giving up.

This shift from chasing perfection to honoring progress will shape every step forward from here on out.

Recovery Drives: Rebuilding Confidence Gently

After a tough setback, don't force yourself straight back into high-stress routes. Instead, try a **recovery drive**—a safe, simple outing meant to reconnect with driving on your own terms. That could mean driving just around the block, sitting in the car with the engine running, or picking a quiet neighborhood street.

Keep expectations light. If anxiety spikes, pause or turn back. Celebrate the fact that you tried, no matter how small the step. Recovery drives slowly shrink fear's power, helping you prove to yourself that one rough outing doesn't erase all your progress.

Knowing When to Pause—and When to Push Forward

An important part of building confidence is balancing rest and challenge. Some days, you'll need to pause—especially if anxiety stays high despite practice, or if life stress leaves you exhausted. Other days, curiosity or boredom signals it's time to stretch yourself a little further.

Pause if you notice:

- Persistent fatigue or irritability.
- Anxiety that remains high drive after drive.
- Major life stressors draining your energy.

Push forward if you notice:

- Routine drives feel easy or dull.
- Curiosity about new routes grows.
- Low anxiety before and during drives.

By listening to your body and mind, you prevent burnout and keep momentum sustainable.

Before moving on, take a moment to notice how your thinking has started to shift already. You've begun laying the groundwork for steady improvement—one flexible goal at a time. In the next chapter, we'll dig into practical ways to prepare before each drive so your mindset and environment set you up for calm and confidence from the start.

Chapter 3: Immediate Tools for In-the-Moment Panic

The Pull-Over Protocol: Steps for Safe Pausing During Panic

Picture this: You're on the road, traffic humming around you, and suddenly your chest tightens. Your hands tremble on the wheel. The world seems to shrink to the inside of your car. You might hear your thoughts go wild—"What if I can't keep control? What if something bad happens right now?" If panic has ever crept up on you while driving, you know the urge to escape is powerful and immediate. What's often missing in these moments is a trusted plan—a clear set of steps to follow when panic tries to hijack your drive. Knowing exactly what to do can cut through the fog and give you back a sense of control.

This is where the Pull-Over Protocol comes in. Having a reliable method for pulling over safely is not just about getting off the road. It's about giving yourself permission to pause, catch your breath, and regain composure, all while staying safe. When you know you have an exit strategy, much of the fear about "what if I panic?" loses its power. This plan isn't just for worst-case scenarios; it's a tool you can use any time things feel overwhelming.

First, when you notice that rising panic, start by scanning for a safe place to pull over. Don't rush—give yourself time to look for an area away from fast-moving traffic. Rest areas, parking lots, wide residential streets or an immediate shoulder if need be are all good options. Even a side street or a well-lit gas station can work in a pinch. Don't worry about looking "strange" to others; your safety comes first. Once you spot your spot, signal early so drivers around you know your intentions. Ease off the gas gently—there's no need to slam on the brakes. The goal is to keep things steady, smooth, and predictable for both yourself and anyone behind you.

After you've come to a full stop, shift into park. If you're on the side of a busy road or in a questionable area, flip on your hazard lights so other drivers give you space. If it helps you feel more grounded, turn off the engine, but leave your lights on if it's dark or rainy. Now, let yourself sit back in the seat. Take stock: You're safe, out of traffic, and nobody's rushing you. Remind yourself that stopping isn't failing—it's smart self-awareness in action. Even seasoned drivers pause when they need to regroup.

Repeat this affirmation aloud or in your head: "Pausing is a skill, not a setback." Some of my clients even write this on an index card and keep it in the visor as a gentle reminder that stopping is strength in disguise. Taking a break doesn't erase progress—it builds trust with yourself and shows that you can respond wisely even when anxiety tries to take over.

Now that you're safely parked, use a self-soothing script to bring your mind and body back to baseline. Try saying quietly: *"I am safe. I can take as long as I need right here."* You might close your eyes for a moment, notice the feel of the seat beneath you, or place your hand on your heart if that helps calm racing thoughts. Remind yourself that there's no timer running; this space belongs to you until you're ready to continue.

Plenty of people worry about what happens if someone approaches while they're pulled over—maybe another driver or even a police officer asks if everything's okay. You don't owe anyone a detailed explanation. A simple script works wonders: *"I just needed a moment to regroup, thank you."* Most people will nod and move along, or offer a quick word of support.

If a police officer approaches and your car isn't in an approved parking zone, they may ask you to move. Officers are usually friendly and understanding—

simply thank them, then relocate your vehicle to a safer or designated spot before continuing your break.

If someone seems overly curious or persistent, repeat your response with calm confidence: *"I'm fine, just taking a break."* Trust that it's perfectly normal to pause when you need it.

Interactive Element: Pull-Over Protocol Reflection

Take out your phone or a notepad and jot down your own version of the Pull-Over Protocol. Where could you safely pull over in your usual driving areas? Write out your preferred self-soothing script and keep it handy next drive. Personalizing this protocol increases your readiness and helps anchor calm when anxiety rises.

Remember, having a plan for pausing is not just about dealing with panic—it's about taking back control from fear and making driving work for you again.

Mindful Breathing on the Road: Three Proven Techniques

Stress can easily find you on the road—tightening breath, a racing heart, and tense hands on the wheel. This is your body's stress response, but you can disrupt it right where you sit. Intentional breathing does more than provide calm; it signals your nervous system to regulate itself, slowing adrenaline and bringing you back to your baseline. The key is having a few reliable techniques that are easy to remember, even in stressful driving moments. Here are three research-backed methods you can use without ever taking your eyes off the road.

First is box breathing, or four-square breathing, which provides structure and steadies both mind and body. Picture a box: inhale for four counts, hold for four, exhale for four, hold again for four. You might imagine tracing the box with your finger on the steering wheel. Breathe in through your nose—one, two, three, four—hold for four, exhale slowly through your mouth—one, two, three, four—hold again for four, then repeat until you feel calmer. This rhythm slows and regulates your breathing, lowering your heart rate and helping ease symptoms like racing thoughts or tingling. If you worry about forgetting the sequence, jot "In-2-3-4, Hold-2-3-4, Out-2-3-4, Hold-2-3-4" on a sticky note by your dashboard.

The second technique, extended exhale breathing, helps when anxiety causes you to over-breathe and feel lightheaded. It works by making your exhale longer than your inhale. Inhale through your nose for a count of four, then exhale gently through your mouth for a count of six. Think of blowing through a straw to stretch out the exhale. Longer exhalations reassure your body, cueing it to shift out of "fight or flight." Your shoulders and jaw may relax as carbon dioxide levels rebalance. This approach is especially useful if you feel short of breath or panicky in stop-and-go traffic. If counting is tough when you're tense, use a mental prompt like "Breathe in...slow out...".

The third approach, anchor breath, incorporates a simple physical cue to ground you during spikes of anxiety. Choose a movement—like pressing your palm against the steering wheel or resting your hand on your thigh. Each inhale, squeeze or press down; each exhale, release and soften your grip. This tactile focus ties your attention to the here and now, helping channel restless energy and providing a sense of control. If you tend to dissociate or feel spacey during panic episodes, anchor breath offers a concrete way back to yourself.

All three techniques work by stimulating the vagus nerve, a major player in calming the nervous system. Slow, purposeful breathing reduces excess adrenaline and soothes the conversation between brain and body, resulting in fewer palpitations, less dizziness, and a stronger sense of stability, even when anxiety strikes.

As you practice, you may find your mind wandering or doubting the process—this is normal. If you get distracted, gently return to counting or focusing on your breath or touch cue, without criticism. Pairing breathing with a calming sensory anchor—like a bit of lavender oil on a tissue or a soothing car freshener—can enhance the effect, connecting scent and steady breath.

At times, anxiety may linger after several rounds of breathing. This doesn't mean your efforts failed; every pause you take interrupts the stress spiral, even if just a little. Practice these techniques during regular drives as well as during tense moments—over time, they'll become more automatic and effective when you truly need them.

Visual Reminder: Quick Breathing Diagram

Draw a simple box on an index card:

Top—Inhale 4 | Right—Hold 4 | Bottom—Exhale 4 | Left—Hold 4

Place it somewhere visible in your car as a subtle reminder to practice whenever you need some steadiness at the wheel.

Grounding Exercises for When You Feel Out of Control

When panic creeps in while you're driving, your thoughts can spin so fast that the road fades into the background. Maybe you start to feel disconnected, as if you're floating above your own body, or as if the world outside your windshield isn't quite real. This is what many call "being in your head"—caught in a loop of spiraling worries and physical sensations that feed each other. Grounding is how you break that loop. Grounding pulls your awareness out of those racing thoughts and anchors it firmly in the here and now, in your body and in the moment. It's a lifeline for when you feel spaced out, trapped outside reality, or on the edge of losing control.

One of the most reliable grounding methods is the "5-4-3-2-1" sensory scan. It works by shifting your focus to what's physically real around you, instead of what's swirling in your mind. As you drive—or even when you're waiting at a stop—you simply name five things you can see. This could be a red car, a billboard, a tree swaying by the road, a cracked section of pavement, or sunlight on your dashboard. Next, move to four things you can feel: the curve of the wheel under your hands, the texture of your seat, cool air from the vent, or your shoes pressing against the pedals. Then, focus on three things you hear—the hum of the engine, music on the radio, distant sirens. Two things you can smell might include the faint scent of coffee or a hint of car freshener. Finally, one thing you can taste—perhaps a lingering mint or just the dryness in your mouth. Move through these steps slowly. The process is like a mental anchor; each sense brings you closer to what's real right now.

Tactile grounding is another favorite because it gives your hands something to do and makes you aware of the physical space you occupy. Reach out and touch something with texture—a beaded keychain, a ridged steering wheel cover, even your jeans or a bracelet. Let yourself really notice the temperature, shape, or firmness beneath your fingers. If your mind tries to race ahead, bring it back to this sensation: "I feel the pattern of my steering wheel. I notice the warmth from my palm." The goal isn't to analyze but to notice. This is about being present in your body instead of lost in your head.

These grounding techniques are especially handy during situations that tend to trigger feelings of unreality. For example, maybe traffic stops unexpectedly on the freeway and suddenly you sense yourself detaching—almost as if you're watching someone else drive. Or perhaps crossing a long bridge makes everything feel dreamlike and distant, intensifying anxiety. Grounding cuts through that haze and brings clarity back to your senses. If traffic is stalled and you notice yourself drifting away mentally, start with a prompt: "What's one color I see out the window right now?" Name it—blue car, green sign—and then pick another. String together these tiny observations until you feel more solid.

Sometimes unreal sensations pop up when driving through tunnels or parking garages where lighting is odd or sounds echo strangely. In those moments, ask yourself: "Can I feel my feet pressing on the floor mat?" Press down gently, wiggle your toes, notice the resistance underfoot. Even shifting slightly in your seat can help remind your nervous system that you are right here, not somewhere far away.

Being present in your body doesn't mean ignoring anxiety—it means refusing to let it take over completely. When grounding feels awkward at first, keep going; it's a skill that sharpens with use. Try small mental scripts like: "I am noticing what's real in this moment," or "My senses are helping me stay present." If words escape you, just repeat what you see or feel out loud or silently.

People sometimes worry about appearing strange if someone catches them talking quietly or touching objects more than usual. You don't have to narrate everything aloud—these prompts work silently too. In fact, most drivers are too busy with their own commutes to notice what you're doing anyway.

What matters most is that grounding disrupts panic before it spirals further. The difference between "being in your head" and "being in your body" is often all it takes to steer yourself back toward calm. Even if anxiety lingers, these techniques make sure it doesn't run the whole show.

Interactive Prompt: Sensory Menu Practice

Next time you park or wait at a light, mentally list three things for each sense before moving again—sight, touch, sound. This not only builds your grounding muscle for stressful drives but helps connect calm to these everyday moments behind the wheel.

The "Red Light Reset": Calming Tools at Stoplights

Red lights have a reputation for triggering anxiety. You're stuck, unable to move forward, watching the seconds tick away while your mind races. Maybe you scan the cross-traffic and feel your chest tighten, or you worry about holding up the line behind you. But what if these moments could actually work in your favor? Think of every red light as a scheduled break—a built-in pause where you get to breathe, regroup, and reconnect with yourself before hitting the gas again. Rather than treating stoplights as traps, try using them as reset points. Repeat quietly: "Red lights are my chance to reset, not a trap." This simple phrase can flip the script on what used to feel like a threat.

You only need thirty or sixty seconds to release tension and lower anxiety. One of the quickest techniques is micro-breathing. All you do is take two slow, gentle inhales through your nose, filling your lungs but not forcing anything. Then, exhale twice as slowly through your mouth, letting your shoulders drop with each out-breath. These short cycles work because they slow your pulse, disrupt panicked thinking, and give your nervous system a chance to recalibrate. You're not trying to force calm—just giving your body a little space to recover.

Another favorite is quick progressive muscle relaxation. While stopped at the light, grip the steering wheel firmly for a count of five, feeling the tension build in your hands and forearms. Then let go completely, letting your fingers loosen and noticing the warmth that follows. Try this one or two times before the light turns green. Many drivers don't realize how much tension they hold in their hands; this simple clench-and-release not only breaks up anxious energy but also makes you more aware of the present moment.

If you find yourself zoning out or drifting into anxious loops, anchor your attention visually or physically. Place a small sticker, charm, or colorful bead somewhere on your dashboard or steering wheel—a private cue for yourself. When you see it at a red light, let it remind you: "This is my reset moment." The tactile feel of that object under your thumb or forefinger can ground you instantly, especially when words slip away and your thoughts feel crowded.

Stoplights are everywhere—city streets, suburban intersections, even sleepy country roads—and each one offers a fresh chance to practice staying steady in stressful situations. I've worked with people who used to dread rush hour because of the frequent stopping and starting. A former student described feeling trapped by gridlock; her anxiety would snowball with every red light until she felt she couldn't breathe. She started using each stop as a cue for micro-breathing and hand relaxation, pairing them with a favorite song on the radio. Over time, these little resets helped her break the cycle of escalating panic, turning red lights from dreaded obstacles into welcome pauses.

If your mind tries to convince you that everyone is watching, remember how common it is for drivers to fidget at lights—adjusting their seat, checking their mirrors, even stretching out their fingers. No one needs to know what you're doing. You can press your thumb to a sticker or charm, take a breath, or flex your hands without drawing attention.

Sometimes anxiety spikes not from fear of driving itself but from the sense of being boxed in—unable to escape if panic hits at a stoplight. When that thought pops up, respond with gentle logic. Remind yourself: "Lights change quickly. I always have options." If you really need a longer pause, it's perfectly okay to pull onto a side street when safe and take more time for yourself.

It's natural to feel impatient or even frustrated if anxiety doesn't disappear after one red light reset. Progress happens in increments—a little less tension in your jaw this time, an easier inhale next time. The more you practice these quick resets, the more automatic they become. Over time, your brain starts to associate red lights not with dread but with relief—a reliable cue that help is just seconds away.

If you struggle to remember these tools in the moment, try leaving yourself friendly reminders. Write "RESET" on a sticky note and stick it near your speedometer, or set a calming wallpaper on your phone that you'll see when stopped. Some find it helpful to keep a favorite affirmation where it's always in sight: "I can use every red light to care for myself."

Even if traffic is heavy and the day feels overwhelming, every stoplight is another opportunity for self-kindness and calm. Your toolbox of micro-breathing, muscle relaxation, and small tactile cues is always available—and with practice, these resets become a quiet superpower that helps you navigate whatever the road throws your way.

Creating a Personalized "Panic Page" for Your Glovebox

If there's one thing I've noticed over years of working with anxious drivers, it's that panic doesn't wait for the perfect moment. It can show up when you least expect it—maybe during a routine drive or smack in the middle of a crowded intersection. In those split seconds, remembering what helps feels just out of reach. That's why having a personalized "Panic Page" can make all the difference. Think of it as your quick-access emergency guide, right at your fingertips. No need to scramble through your mind or your phone for relief. Everything you need is right there—clear, simple, and tailored to you.

Start by dividing your Panic Page into three sections. The first is a list of your favorite grounding methods and breathing exercises. This isn't about packing the page with every strategy you've ever read; it's about picking two or three that have actually worked for you, even for just a moment. Maybe you like naming objects in your environment, counting slow breaths, or focusing on the feeling of the seat beneath you. Write these out in your own words, as if you were talking to yourself on a tough day. For instance, "Take three slow breaths and feel my hands on the wheel," or "Notice five things I see— traffic lights, signs, clouds, my shoes, dashboard." Keep instructions brief and direct—you want to glance at this page and know exactly what to do.

The next section is all about self-compassion. Here's where you place three scripts or affirmations that really speak to you. These are phrases that cut through the noise of self-doubt and replace it with reassurance. No need for grand declarations—authentic words work best. You might use, "I've been through this before and made it through," or "It's okay to pause—I'm allowed to take up space." Another favorite is, "This feeling is temporary; my safety comes first." These reminders offer comfort when panic tells you otherwise. The more personal they feel, the better they'll work when anxiety runs high.

Your last section is practical but powerful: emergency contacts or support people. Sometimes just seeing a name or number on paper reminds you that connection exists beyond the stress swirling in your mind. Write down your go-to person's name and their phone number. You might add a simple plan: "If I need help, I'll call/text [Name]." This isn't just for emergencies—it's for moments when reassurance from someone who cares can steady your nerves. If calling isn't possible, even reading their name can be grounding.

Personalization matters here. Your Panic Page should reflect your own voice and coping style, not anyone else's. Some people like to type their page and print it out, while others write it by hand for an added sense of ownership. Laminating the card makes it durable—perfect for gloveboxes or pockets where spills and wear are inevitable. If you're more digital, save your Panic Page as a note on your phone or as a PDF that's easy to pull up with one tap. The important thing is that it's easy to find when you need it most.

Here are some templates and examples from drivers I've coached:

- "If I panic, I will read this card and remind myself I'm safe."
- "Breathe in slowly for four counts, out for six."
- "My safe person: Jordan (555-1234)."
- "I survived panic last week—I can get through this too."
- "It's okay to stop if I need to."

Try reviewing your Panic Page before each drive, not just in anxious moments. Read it aloud at home or quietly in the car before you start the engine. This practice helps wire the steps into your memory so they come more naturally under stress. The more familiar you are with your Panic Page, the quicker you'll reach for it when nerves kick up.

You don't have to wait for panic to strike before practicing with this tool. Take time each week to update or tweak your scripts and exercises based on what's working now. Maybe after a few drives you realize certain affirmations don't hit home anymore—swap them out for new ones that fit better. Make this page evolve with you.

A Panic Page is not magic—anxiety may still come knocking—but it gives you structure when everything feels chaotic. The act of preparing this page sends a message to yourself: I'm not powerless here. Even during tough drives, you hold helpful strategies in the palm of your hand.

As we close this chapter, remember that these tools aren't just for emergencies—they're building blocks for long-term confidence behind the wheel. Soon we'll explore how preparing ahead of time can make even tough drives less intimidating and more manageable. You're building habits that support not just crisis moments but every mile ahead.

7

Chapter 4: Building Your Confidence Toolkit—Before You Drive

Visualization Exercises: Calm Rehearsal Before You Get In the Car

You know that tense moment when you're not even in the car yet, but your mind is already busy with what could go wrong? Maybe your shoulders get tight before you even grab your keys, or you catch yourself rehearsing every possible mistake you might make out there on the road. This is where visualization comes in—a tool that's simple, portable, and surprisingly powerful for people like you who want to drive with less fear and more confidence. Picture athletes before a big game: eyes closed, imagining every move. They aren't just daydreaming. They're training their brains to react calmly and confidently under pressure. Visualization is their secret weapon, and it can become yours too.

Let's dig into the science a little, because it's both fascinating and reassuring. When you mentally rehearse a task—like picturing yourself driving calmly down a street—your brain fires up many of the same neural pathways as it does during the real thing. It's called neuroplasticity: your brain's ability to rewire itself with practice, whether that practice happens in your body or just in your mind. Many therapists and coaches use mental rehearsal to help people overcome anxiety, boost performance, and process fears before they ever take action in real life. In fact, research in sports and therapy shows that consistent visualization changes your brain's response to stress, making calm feel familiar instead of foreign. The more vividly you imagine a positive driving experience, the more your mind believes you can actually pull it off.

Try this guided script before your next drive, either sitting comfortably at home or in the driver's seat with the engine off. Close your eyes if you feel safe to do so, or let your gaze soften. Take a slow breath in. Picture yourself opening the car door, sliding into the seat. Imagine how the fabric feels beneath you, how your back settles into place. Notice the steering wheel under your hands— your grip is gentle but steady. Imagine the weight of the keys and the quiet click as they turn in the ignition. Visualize your breath staying slow and even, your shoulders loose. In this scene, you feel safe—your heart rate is steady, and a wave of calm spreads from your chest down to your fingertips. You check your mirrors with ease, start the car, and feel settled—not rushed or on edge.

Now let's rehearse a situation that often causes worry: merging onto a highway. In your mind's eye, watch yourself signaling, checking your mirrors, and smoothly accelerating onto the ramp. You see other cars around you, but instead of panic, you sense focus and control. Your breathing is steady. You merge into traffic with space to spare. There's no racing heartbeat—just a quiet confidence that you know what to do next.

If anxious thoughts interrupt—maybe you hear that old "what if I panic" voice in your head—notice it without judgment and gently bring yourself back to the scene. It's normal for worry to intrude at first. When it happens, silently repeat: "I am safe here. I am practicing calm." Over time, this redirection becomes automatic, helping you stay anchored in positive imagery.

Building visualization into your routine makes it most effective. You don't need a fancy setup or lots of extra time. Try visualizing calm while sipping your morning coffee or tea—just two minutes spent picturing yourself driving with ease can set a positive tone for the day. If you're planning a drive later, set a gentle reminder on your phone: "Pause and visualize." Even a brief mental rehearsal before stepping out the door can make a difference.

For those who want an extra boost, pairing visualization with a calming scent or object creates multi-sensory reinforcement. Hold a favorite stone, soft fabric, or even dab a bit of lavender oil on your wrist while you visualize driving calmly. This ties physical sensation to mental rehearsal, making the sense of calm stickier and easier to recall when anxiety rises for real.

Interactive Element: Visualization Habit Tracker

Draw a simple chart with seven boxes—one for each day of the week. Each time you practice visualization (even for two minutes), check off a box and jot down one word about how you felt afterward: "settled," "hopeful," "nervous but tried." At the end of the week, notice patterns—did practicing make it easier to approach real drives? Did your worries shrink even a little? This small act of tracking progress keeps motivation up and helps you see subtle but important shifts over time.

Visualization won't erase all anxiety overnight, but it lays down new tracks in your mind—tracks where calm and control feel possible again. You're not just hoping things will get better; you're training your brain to believe that they actually can.

Car Setup for Comfort and Confidence

Everything inside your car—from the position of your seat to the clutter on the dash—affects how calm or anxious you feel while driving. Small discomforts can build tension, while a well-arranged space helps your body relax and your mind stay clear.

Before driving, do a quick "comfort scan":

- **Seat and mirrors:** Adjust your seat so your back is supported, knees slightly bent, and feet reach pedals without strain. Set the headrest at the right height and position mirrors so you see clearly without twisting.
- **Climate:** Set the temperature and airflow for comfort. Air that is too cold, hot, or blowing in your face adds stress.
- **Clutter:** Clear out extra cups, receipts, or bags. A tidy space reduces visual chaos and helps you feel more grounded.

Add small comforts that work for you. A soft steering wheel cover can make driving feel less tense, and calming scents like lavender or citrus can ease stress. Affirmation cards with short phrases such as "I can do this" offer quick reassurance when nerves rise. Some drivers keep a grounding object, like a smooth stone or beads, to hold at red lights or during anxious moments.

Personal rituals can also bring calm. Wiping the dashboard before each drive, carrying a familiar water bottle, or putting on sunglasses before leaving the driveway can become simple signals of safety and readiness. These routines reinforce a sense of control and help settle anxiety before it builds.

Over time, these habits reshape how you experience your car. Instead of being a place that triggers stress, it becomes a space you've customized for comfort, calm, and confidence—one you know how to return to whenever driving feels overwhelming.

Crafting a Calming Driving Playlist

Music can calm nerves, steady breathing, and relax tense muscles, making it a powerful tool for easing driving anxiety. The right playlist isn't just distraction—sound directly affects your nervous system, helping shift stress into calm focus.

Build your playlist around familiarity and comfort. Choose slower tempos, soft vocals, or instrumentals without sudden changes. Avoid aggressive tracks, news, or talk radio that can spike tension. Classical, ambient, or acoustic music works well for relaxation, while mellow pop can gently lift low energy. Nature sounds—rain, waves, birds—also mask traffic noise and create a peaceful atmosphere.

Make the playlist part of your routine. Start drives with a "confidence anthem," or use calming tracks alongside breathing exercises. A three-minute song can guide slow, steady breaths at red lights or before pulling out, eventually becoming a cue for relaxation.

Keep your playlists flexible: one for anxious days, another for low energy, and one for pure nature sounds. Refresh them regularly and hold onto "anchor songs" that always help. Some people end each drive with a specific track as closure, marking another successful trip.

Your car's audio system can be more than entertainment—it can be a tool for creating control, comfort, and confidence every time you drive.

Pre-Drive Check-Ins: Tracking Your Mood and Readiness

Supporting yourself before driving often starts with a simple pause to assess how you feel. Instead of automatically heading out, take a moment to notice your energy, mood, and physical state. This isn't about overthinking; it's about self-awareness—a key tool against overwhelming anxiety in the car. A quick self-check can help you avoid those "in over my head" moments that can sometimes snowball into panic. Making this a habit helps you manage anxiety, adjust your plans, and approach driving with intention, not dread.

Begin with an easy self-assessment. Rate your current anxiety from one to ten. Are you at a two or three, feeling only mildly nervous, or is stress pushing you to a seven or eight? Pinpointing your number won't fix everything, but it helps reveal patterns. Then ask: have you eaten or had water recently? Hunger or dehydration often worsens anxiety—sometimes a snack or drink quickly improves things. Also consider whether you're rested; exhaustion raises your stress and reduces focus. These quick check-ins help you meet your needs before you drive.

Other helpful questions include: Did anything upsetting happen today? Are you in a rush? Did you take your medication? Recently have you had caffeine or sugar? Such small details can shape your resilience on the road. Taking inventory gives you options, reminding you that you don't always have to push through if it doesn't feel right.

Next, use your check-in results to guide your choices. If your anxiety is a six or above, do a short breathing exercise before starting the engine—even a few minutes can help. If you haven't eaten, grab a snack first. If you're extremely tired, stick to an easy route or delay your trip. On tough days, consider asking for support—maybe have someone ride along, or call a friend first. Sometimes it's best to postpone a non-essential drive altogether.

With this practice, you'll sometimes recognize red flags and simplify your plans, choosing a brief drive around the block over a long trek. Other days, you'll feel ready to stretch your boundaries. The goal isn't to eliminate discomfort, but to avoid pushing yourself into situations that erode your confidence. Checking in lets you plan drives that match your current capacity.

To make this a routine, create a simple mood and readiness checklist on paper or in your phone notes. For example:

- Anxiety level (1–10):
- Did I eat and hydrate?
- Did I rest?
- Is my body tense or relaxed?
- Am I feeling rushed or calm?
- What's one thing I can do if I get stressed while driving?

Run through this list before each drive, even if it's just in your head. Jot down the date, your answers, and how the drive went. For example: "Anxiety 6/10, skipped breakfast, tired." You might choose to eat first and then drive only as far as a nearby store, making the trip manageable instead of overwhelming.

Reflecting on these notes over time helps spot trends. You might see that skipping lunch always raises your anxiety on the ride home, or that certain days are harder due to external stress. Patterns will reveal what works best for you, such as: "When I check in and adjust my plans, driving feels smoother." Over time, this helps you trust your judgment.

Here's a simple tracker template:

Date/Mood Rating (*1–10) Drive Outcome/What Helped/Hindered

04/12/24 *7 Short drive only ate snack first, called friend

04/13/24 *3 Drove new route well-rested, playlist helped

04/14/24 *9 Skipped drive too anxious, rescheduled

This table isn't about being perfect—it encourages awareness and self-kindness. Use it as often as makes sense. Some people track every drive for a while; others use it during difficult periods or after setbacks. Gradually, this builds safer experiences behind the wheel and, more importantly, strengthens your self-trust.

Treating pre-drive check-ins as a regular practice—not just an emergency step—gives you a helpful buffer from panic. You start making driving decisions from a place of genuine self-knowledge, which makes any journey less daunting and much more within your control.

Scheduling Drives for Success: Timing, Routes, and Backups

Finding the right time and place for your drives changes everything when you live with driving anxiety. You don't need to make your life harder by heading out during rush hour or in the middle of a rainstorm. Instead, think of scheduling as one of your strongest tools. When you pick your moments, you regain a sense of control. Start by looking at your daily or weekly routine and noticing which times feel less stressful. Early afternoons often mean lighter traffic, while mid-morning can be calmer than the busy start of the day. Daylight also helps—your mind tends to feel steadier when you can see clearly and don't have to deal with blinding headlights or shadows. If you can, avoid driving right after work or school lets out, since roads fill up with hurried commuters and distracted drivers.

Routes matter just as much as timing. Familiarity brings confidence, so pick roads you know well, at least for now. Driving the same loop again and again isn't boring—it's smart skill-building. You'll notice that predictability gives your nervous system a break, letting your mind focus on staying calm instead of bracing for surprises. Once you feel comfortable, you can gradually introduce new streets or intersections, but there's no rush. It's okay to stick with what feels safe in the beginning.

Not every drive needs to have a destination that's urgent or necessary. Scheduling "exposure drives" gives you a chance to practice without any pressure to perform. Maybe one afternoon you drive around a quiet neighbor-hood just to get the feel of being on the road again. Or you might plan a short trip to a local park where you can turn around easily if you need to. These drives help rewire your associations with being behind the wheel—from dread to something more neutral, or even positive, over time.

Backup plans are your safety net and can make or break your confidence on tougher days. Before each drive, map out an alternate route in case you hit unexpected construction or traffic jams that might spike your anxiety. You can also look up side streets or parking lots along your route where you could pause if things get too intense. Some people find it calming to let a friend or family member know when they're planning to drive, setting up a quick call or text check-in as needed. This way, if anxiety ramps up, you know exactly whom you'll reach out to—and how.

I always recommend having an "if-then" plan for those just-in-case moments. If traffic is crawling and you feel trapped, then take the next exit and find a side street to regroup. If you notice panic building, then pull into a lot or safe spot and use your grounding tools before continuing. Giving yourself options prevents panic from feeling like a dead end.

Getting organized with your drives doesn't have to be complicated. Print out a weekly planner page or create a simple spreadsheet on your phone where you jot down planned drives, start times, chosen routes, and backup options. Add checkboxes for ideal timing ("after lunch"), quick weather checks, and making sure emergency contacts are easy to find in your phone.

If paper planners aren't your thing, digital reminders or apps can work just as well. Set a calendar event for your drive and include notes on timing and routes. Color code high-stress days so you know when to keep things simple, and highlight successful drives for a little boost.

Sometimes things won't go according to plan—and that's okay. The more you practice flexible scheduling and backup planning, the easier it gets to adapt on the fly without feeling like the world is ending. Each drive becomes another chance to build resilience and prove to yourself that even setbacks are survivable.

To wrap up this chapter, remember that smart planning gives anxiety less room to grow. Choosing calmer times and familiar routes lets you build skill without overwhelm, while backup plans soften the fear of getting stuck or trapped. Over time these habits will become smoother, giving you more freedom on your own terms. Up next, we'll look closely at what happens in the car—real-time strategies for staying steady and handling whatever comes your way. Your toolkit is growing stronger every time you plan ahead and show up for yourself.

8

Chapter 5: Step-by-Step Gradual Exposure for Real-World Progress

Designing Your Personal Exposure Hierarchy

Imagine standing at the edge of a pool, hesitant to jump straight into the deep end. Instead, you ease in—first your toes, then your feet, then a slow wade. This mirrors gradual exposure for driving anxiety: you don't leap in all at once but build confidence through small, safe steps. Each successful move forward—even tiny ones—adds up, until facing the big fears doesn't seem as daunting.

Tackling all your driving fears at once—like jumping from not driving in months to merging onto a busy highway—is overwhelming and unhelpful. Breaking the process into manageable steps makes it doable. Your first victory might simply be sitting in the car with the engine off, then turning it on and remaining at ease, then backing down the driveway. These aren't trivial; they are real signs of progress. With a personalized plan, known as an exposure hierarchy, you can start exactly where you are—not where anyone else thinks you should be.

To create your exposure ladder, list driving scenarios that make you anxious, ranging from mildly uncomfortable to panic-inducing. These could include:

being a passenger, driving with company, going solo, unfamiliar roads, busy intersections, highways, garages, and even certain weather. Rate each one from 1 to 10, where 1 is minor discomfort ("sitting in my parked car") and 10 is peak anxiety ("highway driving at rush hour"). Don't judge your ratings— they're simply a map of your comfort zones and challenges.

A sample template might look like:

1. Sitting in the car with engine off
2. Engine on, car in park
3. Driving down your street
4. Navigating a quiet block
5. Right turn at a stop sign
6. One-mile drive without stops
7. Merging onto a quiet main road
8. Left turn at an intersection
9. Short drive with a passenger
10. Highway entrance ramp during off-peak hours

To identify your starting point, ask, "Which scenario feels only a bit uncomfortable—not terrifying, yet not effortless?" Begin here. If unsure, imagine advising a friend with your anxieties; often, we're more realistic and compassionate with others.

When your hierarchy is set, define realistic goals for each step, like repeating an action five times until your anxiety decreases noticeably. Repetition— rather than speed—drives progress. If you finish a step still anxious, repeat it before moving on. Confidence builds through frequent, low-pressure practice, not through forcing dramatic leaps.

Stay flexible. Some days, anxiety may spike or you'll need to repeat steps. Life may interfere, or some milestones might be easier than you anticipated. It's normal to adjust or pause. Move at your pace—no outside timeline matters more than your own readiness.

For example, one person I worked with spent weeks practicing right turns at a quiet intersection before tackling left turns or busier roads. At first, she worried she was going too slow, but repetition steadily eased her anxiety. With patience, her confidence grew—each small victory proved worthwhile. There's no race to the finish; it's about increasing ability and ease as you go.

Practicing in Park: Sitting in the Driver's Seat Without Moving

When anxiety is tied to driving, even sitting in your car can feel like a challenge. The first step isn't about moving at all—it's about getting reacquainted with the driver's seat without pressure to go anywhere. Simply sit with the engine off and no destination in mind. This small action helps retrain your nervous system, showing your body that the car doesn't always mean stress.

As you settle in, notice the details around you: the feel of the seat, the texture of the wheel, the light through the windshield. Tune into your senses—what you see, hear, or feel in the moment. Take slow, deep breaths, letting each exhale release tension. If your thoughts race ahead, gently bring them back to a single detail you can observe right now.

A simple grounding script can help: *"I am here in my car. I am safe. There is nothing I need to do right now."* Speak it quietly or silently until the words begin to feel steady.

Track your anxiety level before and after. Even a small shift—a drop from an 8 to a 6—is progress. Repetition is key; the more often you practice, the more natural it feels. Add variety by sitting at different times of day, with or without music, or with a trusted friend nearby. Each variation builds flexibility and confidence.

This exercise isn't about pushing through discomfort but about noticing when comfort grows. Over time, sitting in your parked car shifts from a source of dread to a place of calm, creating the foundation for every step that follows.

Driver's Seat Calm Log

Use this log to track your progress each time you practice.

- **Date/Time:** _____
- **Before rating (1–10):** _____
- **After rating (1–10):** _____
- **Notes (what I noticed, what helped, what felt different):**

Low-Stress Loops: Mastering Quiet Neighborhood Drives

Once you're comfortable in the driver's seat, the next step is moving in a safe, low–pressure space. Quiet residential streets or empty parking lots are ideal—minimal traffic, wide lanes, and room to breathe. Think of these areas as training grounds where the goal is progress, not perfection. Plan a short loop of three or four blocks, or circle a lot during a quiet time. Knowing your route helps reduce uncertainty.

Before moving, settle into your routine: adjust mirrors, buckle up, and take a slow breath. Start the car, check your surroundings, and ease forward with light pressure on the pedals. Keep your speed low, focus on steady breathing, and signal turns well in advance. Each stop is a chance to pause and move only when ready.

After completing a loop, return to your starting point, shift into park, and notice how your body feels. Was your breathing easier? Did your grip relax? Log each attempt—what went smoothly, what felt tough. Over time, these notes reveal progress you might otherwise miss.

Obstacles will appear, even on quiet roads. If another car approaches, slow down, pull over, and let them pass. If you miss a turn or brake too hard, remind yourself that mistakes are normal—reset and continue when ready. If anxiety spikes, use grounding tools: count houses, loosen your grip, or pull over briefly until calm returns.

Try loops at different times of day to build flexibility. Celebrate every outing, no matter how it felt. Each lap adds confidence, proving you can handle movement behind the wheel at your own pace.

Progress Reflection: Post-Loop Log

After each practice drive, jot down:

- What did I do well today?
- What felt harder than I expected?
- Did I use any coping tools? Which ones worked best?
- What's one thing I want to try again next time?

Your notes become proof that real change is underway—one quiet loop at a time.

Graduating to Busier Streets: Handling Intersections and Lights

Moving from quiet streets to busier roads can feel overwhelming: more engines, unpredictable traffic, pedestrians, traffic lights, and longer lines of cars. That mix of nerves and excitement is normal—it means you're gaining independence one step at a time.

Ease in by adding new elements gradually. Start with a single intersection or a few stoplights during low-traffic times like mid-morning. Begin with right turns, which are easier since traffic comes from one direction. Once comfortable, progress to left turns, where judging safe gaps is key. Take your time—ignore honks or pressure. Your safety is always more important than anyone else's impatience.

Stoplights often trigger anxiety, especially as they change. Remind yourself a red light is just a pause. If tension rises, do a quick "red light reset": inhale slowly, exhale fully, and drop your shoulders. Focus on simple details—the car color ahead, the click of your signal, or the feel of your seatbelt. Grounding in the present helps quiet anxious thoughts.

At four-way stops, slow fully and look left, right, then left again. The first to arrive goes first; if you arrive together, yield to the right. If another driver waves you on, accept with a nod or wave back. Small courtesies make the process smoother.

Roundabouts can seem daunting. Approach slowly, note lane signs, yield to cars already inside, and only enter when there's a clear gap. Keep a steady pace and watch for pedestrians at exits. With practice, roundabouts become predictable.

At pedestrian crossings, scan both sides even when your light is green. People can cross unexpectedly, and not every driver obeys signals. Staying alert helps you feel prepared.

Set small goals, like planning a route with three intersections and two lights. You don't need to feel perfectly calm—just more confident each time. Afterward, jot quick notes about what felt easier or when focus replaced anxiety. These are victories worth noticing.

Use affirmations at busy spots: "I can take my time and wait for a clear, safe gap." Repeating this reinforces patience and trust in yourself.

Mistakes will happen—hesitating too long, stalling at a light, or feeling pressured by drivers behind you. Treat them as lessons, not failures. Reflect briefly, adjust, and keep going.

Each outing on busier streets proves you can handle more than you thought. Celebrate every effort—these steps build the confidence that leads to full independence on the road.

Preparing for Highways, Bridges, and Tunnels—Safely and Gradually

Getting ready for highways, bridges, or tunnels can feel like reaching a new peak in your driving journey. These environments often bring nerves—speed, height, enclosed spaces, or the sense of being trapped. Many new drivers avoid them, convinced they'll never feel calm. But with gradual, thoughtful steps and preparation, these challenges can simply become part of routine driving.

Begin by observing, not driving. Find a highway rest area or park near an on-ramp to watch how traffic flows. Notice merging, lane changes, and the general rhythm. Spend time as a passenger: pay attention to sights and sounds without the pressure of being in control. Note how your body reacts—tension or a knot in your chest is just feedback you'll want to use later.

When ready to move forward, plan your first attempt like you would an important event. Pick a familiar, flat, short stretch of highway, preferably during quieter hours such as early morning or midday on weekends. Good weather helps. Bring a trusted friend or family member, either in the passenger seat or in a car behind you for support. Just knowing someone is near can reduce tension.

Start small: pick an entrance leading to a short section of highway with an easy exit within a mile or two. The goal is simple—merge, stay in the right lane, and exit at the first opportunity. The right lane gives quick access to exits and provides space from faster traffic. Tell yourself that if at any point your anxiety spikes, you can always exit quickly—there's no need to force yourself to stay longer than you want.

Highways are unique: the speed, constant movement, and feeling of not being able to stop. Focus on your controllable actions—steady hands on the wheel and eyes on the road ahead. Don't let impatient drivers behind you get in your head. If your anxiety rises, use grounding routines like deep breathing or repeating a phrase such as "Steady and safe."

Bridges can trigger worries about height or being suspended over water or traffic. When approaching, fix your gaze on the end of the bridge instead of looking down or out. Remind yourself, "This is just another road." Stay steady in your lane and maintain speed. If intrusive "what if" thoughts come up, focus on your breath or calming music instead.

Tunnels may cause discomfort about being enclosed or losing sight of daylight. Before entering, take a few slow breaths and remind yourself this is temporary and safe. While driving through, focus on the taillights ahead or lines on the pavement, not the tunnel's length. If anxiety rises, stick with slow breaths—most tunnels are surprisingly short.

Every bit of progress deserves acknowledgment. Even if you only drive one exit before stopping, that's real progress. Celebrate—send a text, write it in your log, or sit quietly and recognize that you didn't avoid the challenge. If it feels like too much, return to easier steps until you're ready again.

A former client used to avoid bridges at all costs, even altering her schedule by hours. With gentle support from her sister and practice during quiet, early mornings, she slowly built up courage. Over time, she crossed solo, and later, a phone call for support was enough. She honored her pace and gained confidence one step at a time.

Remind yourself: "Every attempt builds my confidence, no matter how small." There's no finish line—just steady growth earned through practice.

After each attempt, pause and reflect—what worked, what was tough, what you'd do differently next time. Use this insight to plan your next step.

This chapter demonstrates how gradual exposure turns daunting places like highways, bridges, and tunnels into manageable parts of driving through patience, preparation, and reflection. Next, we'll discuss building resilience for setbacks and tracking progress so your achievements aren't overshadowed by any bumps along the way.

9

Chapter 6: Cognitive and Mindfulness Strategies for On-the-Road Calm

Spotting "What-If" Thinking—and How to Defuse It

Picture this: you're putting on your seatbelt and, before you even start the engine, your mind starts racing ahead. Without warning, your thoughts latch onto a string of "what-ifs." "What if I get stuck in traffic and panic?" "What if my hands get sweaty and I can't grip the wheel?" "What if something happens with no one around to help?" These questions don't come one at a time—they pile up, fast. If this sounds familiar, you're in good company. This kind of thinking is more than just worry; it's a mental habit that feeds anxiety before your tires even leave the driveway.

"What-if" thinking is at the heart of anticipatory anxiety. This isn't just regular caution or smart planning—it's a loop that plays out worst-case scenarios over and over. Instead of preparing you for real possibilities, it locks you in a cycle of dread. Your brain gets stuck in an endless loop: imagining everything that could go wrong, even if it's unlikely or completely out of your control. This is different from realistic preparation. Planning for rainy weather is healthy; obsessing over "What if I can't breathe while driving on the highway?" keeps your nervous system stuck in high alert. Anticipatory anxiety is sneaky because it happens before you even face the situation. It tricks you into feeling like you're being responsible, but really, it just increases fear and avoidance.

To break this pattern, start by spotting your own "what-if" habits. Pay attention to your thoughts as you get ready to drive, or even days before a big trip. Notice when you start a sentence in your head with "what if..."—that's a red flag. Maybe it's "What if I miss my exit and get lost?" or "What if I embarrass myself if I need to pull over?" These thoughts don't mean anything bad will happen; they're just mental chatter that your brain has learned over time.

Interactive Exercise: Your "What-If" Checklist

Take a minute, either now or before your next drive, and jot down the top five "what-if" worries that pop up for you. Here are some common ones from drivers I've worked with:

- What if I freeze up at a stoplight?
- What if my car breaks down on the highway?
- What if I have to drive somewhere new and get lost?
- What if someone honks at me and I panic?
- What if my anxiety gets so bad I have to call for help?

Once you've got your list, notice how often these show up. Sometimes, just seeing them written down helps create distance from them—they're not facts, just thoughts.

Now, let's talk about how to defuse these thoughts before they spiral into full-blown anxiety. The first step is to name the thought out loud or in your head: "That's a 'what-if' thought." This simple act gives you a little breathing room. Next, label it for what it is—a worry, not a prediction. Remind yourself: "This is my brain trying to protect me by imagining every possible problem." Finally, gently redirect your focus back to what's actually happening right now. Instead of following the anxious story, look around and notice something real: your hands on the wheel, the color of the dashboard, the feel of the seat beneath you.

Let me share a couple of quick stories from people who used this defusion process during real drives. One parent I worked with feared panicking while taking her kids to school. Her mind would shout, "What if I panic and scare them?" She learned to notice that script, respond with, "There's my 'what-if' again," and then shift her focus to her daughter's favorite song playing. The ride didn't have to be perfect—just more grounded in reality than in fear.

Another driver commuted daily on a busy highway and constantly worried, "What if my car breaks down and I'm stranded?" Instead of arguing with his brain or trying to force the thought away, he'd say, "That's the same old 'what-if' my mind likes to play," then check his dashboard for any real issues. Seeing nothing was wrong brought him back to the present moment. The anxiety didn't vanish instantly, but it stopped running the show.

Defusing "what-if" thinking isn't about making all anxious thoughts disappear forever. It's about noticing them early, naming them without judgment, and returning your attention to what's actually happening—not what might happen someday. The more you practice this process, the easier it becomes to keep those spirals from taking over your drive.

Cognitive Reframing for Catastrophic Thoughts

When driving anxiety sets in, thoughts often leap straight to disaster: spinning out on ice, freezing at an intersection, or losing control in traffic. Catastrophic thinking paints every unknown as danger. It's not just worry over a missed turn—it's the belief that one slip will cause a crash, humiliation, or the end of your ability to drive. The more you listen, the more each drive feels like a gamble.

These all-or-nothing thoughts show up right when reassurance is needed. Maybe it's, "If I panic, I'll lose control," or, "If traffic is heavy, I'll be trapped." Your brain is wired to scan for threats, but it often confuses fear with fact. Most of these predictions never come close to happening.

Reframing means pausing to challenge the story your mind is spinning. Ask:

"Is this a fact, or just a fear?" Then break it down with three questions: What's the worst-case scenario? The best case? The most likely outcome? Writing these out helps. For example: Worst case—"I panic and need to pull over." Best case—"The drive is smooth and I feel proud." Most likely—"I'll feel nervous, but use my tools and arrive safely."

Having ready statements helps too. If you think, "If I panic, I'll crash," counter with, "Panic feels scary, but I've always gotten through it." If you fear traffic, reframe with, "Traffic is uncomfortable, not dangerous. I can always slow down or exit." And if you make a mistake, remind yourself, "Everyone makes mistakes—one slip doesn't mean I'm unsafe." These lines don't erase fear, but they keep perspective and stop anxiety from snowballing.

Practice in calm settings first. Sit in your parked car, notice an anxious thought, then reframe it. Try it before exposure drives too: write your top fear, then two alternate views—one hopeful, one neutral. For example, "I'll panic in traffic" becomes "I may get anxious, but I can slow my breathing," or "If needed, I'll pull over."

With repetition, reframing becomes second nature. Each time you question a catastrophic thought, you show your brain that not every fear deserves airtime. Over time, the "scary movie" fades, replaced with real life—imperfect but manageable.

Mindful Attention: Staying Present, Not Hypervigilant

One of the most important skills for anxious drivers is learning to stay present. But presence doesn't mean being on high alert. There's a big difference between mindful attention and anxious hypervigilance. Mindful attention means gently tuning into the drive, noticing your senses and surroundings without gripping tension. Hypervigilance feels like standing guard—constantly checking mirrors, anticipating dangers, muscles tight, and breath shallow. Instead of driving, you're braced for threats that rarely come.

Think back to a smooth drive where you enjoyed music or scenery, then compare it to one where you scanned mirrors obsessively—that's the contrast. Anxiety pushes your nervous system into overdrive, while mindfulness roots you in the moment: the feel of the wheel, the hum of tires, what's happening now—not what might go wrong.

It may feel odd at first if you're used to being hyper-alert, but with practice it becomes easier—even calming. Try a simple "Noticing Three Things" exercise. Pause to mentally name three things you see, three you hear, and three you feel. The goal isn't to analyze, but to anchor your attention. If anxiety rises mid-drive, redirect focus to a physical sensation: your hand on your chest, the pedal under your foot, or your back against the seat.

A quick mental reset is repeating: "Right now, I am safe and moving forward." Pair it with a slow breath to settle nerves at a red light or during a merge. These small practices keep you grounded, leaving less space for anxious spirals.

One student once managed a rainy, traffic-heavy drive—normally panic-inducing—by focusing on raindrop sounds and naming three sights: taillights, dashboard lights, a puddle reflecting lamps. Each time panic thoughts appeared, she returned to her senses. The drive wasn't anxiety-free, but she stayed steady and proud.

Mindful attention isn't about ignoring real risks; it's about balanced awareness—alert, but not consumed by "what-ifs." Hazards like a sudden stop are easier to notice when you're focused on the present instead of fears or regrets.

You can practice at any point: at stoplights, on quiet stretches, or whenever tension appears. Over time, this shift from hypervigilance to mindful presence makes driving less of a survival test and more of a steady, manageable journey.

Anchoring Techniques for Overwhelm in Unfamiliar Areas

Driving into a new part of town or weaving through a busy city can send a jolt through your system. Even before you reach the first intersection, you might sense nerves creeping up your spine—shoulders stiffen, breath shortens, and that old feeling of wanting to turn back bubbles up. When everything feels foreign, and your mind starts to spin, "anchoring" is your tool for staying steady. In the context of driving anxiety, anchoring means giving yourself a reliable point of focus—something simple, tangible, and within reach—so your attention doesn't scatter all over the place. Think of it like holding on to a sturdy railing when the ground feels unsteady. It can be a word, a sound, a sensation, or even a goalpost along your route. Anchors are not about ignoring your stress; they're about having a touchstone that brings you back to yourself when overwhelm strikes.

I've worked with drivers who swear by repeating a calming word or phrase when everything feels like too much. Something as simple as "steady," "present," or "here and now" whispered under your breath can anchor your thoughts and remind you that you control your pace. I've seen others grip the steering wheel just so—not too tight, but with enough pressure to feel its texture and temperature. Some find the soft click of the turn signal, that familiar tick-tick-tick, is enough to gather scattered thoughts. The beauty of anchoring is that you don't need fancy tools or rare skills; you just need to notice what works for you and bring it into play.

Let's talk toolkit. When those waves of unease start rolling as you cross into an unfamiliar neighborhood or merge onto a busy thoroughfare, try this: pick a single anchor and commit to it for the next few minutes. Maybe it's focusing on the way the steering wheel feels under your palms—notice if it's smooth, textured, warm from the sun, or cool in the shade. If physical sensation isn't doing the trick, repeat your anchor word softly. "Steady." "Calm." "I've got this." Those words aren't magic spells—they just cut through the noise and offer structure to racing thoughts. Others use sound as an anchor: listen to the rhythmic pattern of the turn signal or the gentle hum from the engine. Let these familiar cues remind you that, even in chaos, some things do not change.

For times when overwhelm builds as you navigate new routes or city streets, planning ahead is another anchor. Set your GPS before you leave so you aren't fumbling at every turn. Rather than thinking about the whole route at once, focus only on the next step—"I'm just driving to the next light" or "My only job now is to turn left at Main." Some drivers find that using a specific song helps—pick one track that calms your nerves and play it every time you enter unfamiliar territory. Over time, your mind will associate that song with steadiness and capability, even when everything else feels uncertain.

Landmarks are another powerful anchor for in-the-moment overwhelm. Instead of worrying about the whole journey ahead, pick a visible goal—a blue building at the corner, a gas station sign, a familiar tree—and tell yourself, "I'll drive just to there." Once you reach your landmark, pause mentally and reassess how you feel. Maybe you're ready for another stretch; maybe it's time for a break. This strategy breaks down large tasks into smaller chunks, making them easier to handle.

Anchoring isn't just for use during tense moments; it's also worth reflecting on after you get through a challenging drive in an unfamiliar area. When you park and turn off the engine, take a minute to ask yourself: "What helped me most today?" Did repeating your anchor word keep your hands from shaking? Did focusing on the feel of the steering wheel quiet your racing thoughts? Was it planning your GPS route ahead or choosing a landmark goal that kept you moving forward? Take note of what worked—even if it seemed small—so you'll have an even stronger toolkit next time.

Reflection Prompt

Grab a notebook or your phone and jot down: "Which anchor did I use today? How did it help me in those unfamiliar moments?" Maybe you'll realize one anchor stands out or that you used several together. Over time, this record becomes a collection of victories—small but mighty reminders that you have what it takes to stay steady, even in completely new territory. Anchoring doesn't erase anxiety entirely, but it gives you footing when everything else feels shaky. The more consistently you practice these techniques, the more automatic they'll become—your own quiet arsenal for taking on whatever roads life brings.

Using "Thought Cards" as Quick Reminders in the Car

When anxiety strikes during a drive, your mind can race or go blank, making it tough to recall helpful advice. That's where "thought cards" come in—short, personal reminders you keep close by for stressful moments. While not a magic solution, a thought card interrupts anxious spirals, offering something solid and reassuring when everything else feels overwhelming.

A thought card should be brief, easy to read, and personal. Short cues work especially well because anxiety floods your thoughts, making long advice impossible to recall. Phrases like "I can pause and breathe" or "This feeling will pass" can break through the mental noise. Rather than arguing with your anxiety, these reminders gently ground you, let you slow down, breathe, and focus on the present. They're like a soothing friend in the passenger seat—nonjudgmental, quietly nudging you back on track.

Creating your own thought cards is simple and comforting. Think about your strongest driving worries—panicking in traffic, getting flustered at a stoplight, or making mistakes. Write down three to five honest, supportive phrases in your own words, nothing fancy or forced. Some examples from real drivers: "I can pause and breathe." "This feeling will pass, and I will be okay." "I've handled tough drives before." "You're safe—just drive." "It's okay to pull over if I need to." The best thought cards sound like they're from someone who truly knows you—because they are.

Once you have your phrases, decide where to keep them. Many people laminate their cards and tuck them on the sun visor or dashboard for a quick glance at a stoplight. Others keep them in a cup holder or tape one inside the glove compartment. If paper isn't your style, make them phone wallpapers or save them as notes on your lock screen. Color-coding can help—a red card for panic moments, blue for calming reassurance, green for encouragement when facing something new. Make your reminders both visible and personal, but subtle enough for privacy.

Some drivers rotate cards depending on the day or the drive. If rush hour is stressful, put your strongest calming card up front. For new routes or long trips, try an affirmation like "One mile at a time." You can also use symbols or stickers if words don't resonate—a star for courage, a wave for letting go, a heart for self-compassion.

Here's a brief example: One student dreaded rush hour so much, her stomach would knot up before even getting on the freeway. She created a card reading, "You're safe—just drive," and placed it above her speedometer. When panic threatened to take over, she'd glance at the card, silently repeat the phrase, and focus on her breath. While her fear wasn't erased, having that lifeline kept her from pulling off at every exit, and over time, she began to believe the words.

If you prefer visuals, use bold colors or images to make each card stand out. Laminating makes them durable, or keep them digital for privacy. The key is authenticity—these reminders should be your own words, not generic advice from elsewhere. Let them sound like your voice cutting through anxiety.

Thought cards don't pretend anxiety isn't real. Instead, they give you a steady foothold when things feel shaky. When panic hits, with logic out the window, those simple words can help you ride out the storm and keep moving forward—one block at a time.

As we end this chapter on cognitive and mindfulness tools, remember: each strategy in this section is meant for real-life moments, not just theory. You've learned to spot anxious thought patterns, shift negative thinking, ground yourself in the present, and equip yourself with concrete cues for tough moments. In the next chapter, you'll see how to use these skills in tough driving situations—from freeways to parking lots—so you can meet real-world challenges with growing confidence.

10

Chapter 7: Handling Common Triggers and Tough Situations

Navigating Rush Hour Without Panic

Imagine your phone buzzing with a calendar alert, reminding you to leave if you want to beat morning gridlock. Just thinking about the endless stream of brake lights can make your chest tighten. Maybe you've canceled plans or left late to avoid traffic, only to get caught in a crawl anyway. If so, you're not alone. For many, rush hour isn't just about traffic jams—it's a major stress trigger that magnifies driving anxiety. The unpredictability, slow pace, crowded roads, and feeling boxed in can leave you powerless. However, with the right plan, you can manage these moments instead of letting them control you.

Preparation is essential. Before getting behind the wheel, spend a few minutes running through a rush-hour pre-drive checklist. Don't leave it to chance: open a traffic app like Google Maps or Waze to check live congestion and look for alternate routes, even if they take a bit longer. Sometimes side streets with stop signs are less stressful than highways clogged with impatient drivers. Build in a buffer by leaving twenty or thirty minutes early, so you're not pressed for time. If certain exits are usually jammed, plan to avoid them.

Quickly check items off a list: "Traffic app checked, two route options picked, water bottle filled, playlist ready." These steps give you some control before you start.

While caught in stop-and-go traffic, anxiety can surge. The urge to escape is strong when progress is measured in inches. This is when micro-breathing helps: breathe in for three counts, out for five. Longer exhales trigger relaxation and slow racing thoughts. No need for anything elaborate; just focus on matching your breath to the rhythm of the traffic lights or wipers. Combine this with a self-talk script: "Every car is moving slowly. I am not trapped; I am in control of my space." Repeat it quietly when frustration or panic appear. Remember, everyone around you is also stuck—most drivers feel the same way.

Delays are part of rush hour: long lights, creeping forward, and sudden stops. Instead of fighting these pauses, make them "reset points." At a red light, check in with your body—drop your shoulders, loosen your grip, and take a slow breath. Keep a small tactile object handy—a smooth stone, textured keychain, or stress ball—to ground your attention if you get fidgety. Distraction helps too: listen to a calming playlist or a gentle audiobook. Choose steady, familiar music to keep nerves steady. If your mind drifts to what could go wrong, anchor yourself by naming things you see outside—a blue truck, a billboard, someone walking a dog.

People have beaten rush hour anxiety by practicing in manageable steps. One reader started by driving just one exit during peak time, parking at a coffee shop, then heading home. The first attempts were tough, but short segments built her confidence until she could handle her full commute without dread. Another parent used quiet neighborhood roads during school pickup, working up to busier intersections. Instead of forcing themselves through everything at once, they tackled it in pieces.

Interactive: Rush Hour Drive Planner

- Open your maps app and preview traffic on your route.
- List two alternate routes (even if longer).
- Set a "leave by" time with a 20–30 minute buffer.

- Choose one calming distraction (music, audiobook, tactile object).
- Write your self-talk script for stressful moments.
- After your drive, note one thing that helped and one thing to try next time.

Rush hour may never be enjoyable, but it doesn't have to keep you off the road. Each bit of practice—even just a block farther—builds your confidence that you can handle whatever comes your way.

Managing Tailgaters, Honking, and Aggressive Drivers

Few things ramp up anxiety faster than a tailgater glued to your bumper or the sudden blare of a horn behind you. You might tense up, grip the wheel tighter, and feel a wave of frustration or fear. Thoughts spin: Why are they so close? Am I driving too slow? Will they try to pass dangerously? Here's the truth: every driver faces these moments, but when you already feel anxious behind the wheel, even small acts of aggression can feel enormous. You do not have to let another driver's impatience dictate your experience. Having a plan makes all the difference.

Tailgaters often seem like they're trying to push you along with sheer willpower. Sometimes they flash lights or swerve, pushing your nerves to the edge. In these moments, use a simple three-step protocol. First, stay calm—remind yourself that their behavior is about them, not you. Take a breath and resist the urge to speed up or slam the brakes. Second, maintain your speed steadily; do not let pressure from behind cause you to rush or make mistakes. This keeps you safe and signals you won't be bullied into going faster than feels right. Third, if you can safely move over, change lanes or pull into a turnout. Let them pass without drama or eye contact. Repeat this affirmation in your mind: "Their urgency is not my emergency." It's surprisingly effective for keeping your sense of control.

Honking can feel like a personal attack, especially when you're already on edge. The loudness jolts your system, and it's easy to think you've messed up or become the target of someone's anger. But in reality, honking is usually about the other person's impatience or distraction—not your worth or skill as a driver. Use this script: "Honking is about their impatience, not my worth as a driver." Say it silently or whisper it if you need reassurance. After a horn blast, ground yourself with a quick sensory check—instead of reacting, notice how your hands feel on the wheel or what you see outside your window. This breaks the mental loop and brings you back to the present moment.

Aggressive drivers—those who gesture wildly, tailgate, cut you off, or shout from open windows—can make any drive feel like a test of nerves. When faced with this behavior, avoid making eye contact or responding in any way. Do not return gestures or shout back. Engaging only fuels their anger and escalates the situation. Instead, focus on your own safety: keep both hands on the wheel, eyes forward, and follow traffic laws closely. If someone continues to harass or follow you, drive toward a well-lit public place or police station rather than home. Your priority is getting out of their way and putting distance between yourself and their anger.

If someone yells at you, resist the urge to explain or defend yourself through the window. Most of the time, their anger isn't really about you—it's about their day, their stress, or something unrelated entirely. Let them move on without giving them any more energy than they deserve. Sometimes this means pulling off at a gas station or rest stop, letting them disappear ahead while you take a breather and steady your nerves.

One reader shared how she once felt frozen when a tailgater began flashing his lights and honking at every stop sign. Instead of panicking, she kept her pace and pulled into a nearby gas station. The aggressive driver sped off, and she spent a few minutes sipping water and listening to music before continuing on her way. That simple act of removing herself from the situation gave her back her power and showed that she could handle even high-stress encounters.

Another commuter told me how city driving used to fill him with dread because of constant honking and impatient gestures at every intersection. Over time, he reframed these sounds as "background city noise"—annoying but not dangerous. He kept his focus on his lane and his destination, letting horns fade into the blur of urban life. It took practice, but each trip became less about what others thought and more about staying calm and getting where he needed to go.

Quick Reference: Three-Step Tailgater Protocol

1. **Stay calm**: Breathe deeply, keep your focus forward—don't let their actions rattle you.
2. **Maintain speed**: Drive steadily; don't speed up to please them.
3. **Change lanes when safe**: Move over smoothly at the first safe spot; let them pass without interaction.

Every driver encounters rude or reckless people sometimes, but your response determines whether stress takes over or confidence grows. You can choose calm over chaos in these moments—even if your heart races and your palms sweat. With every experience handled this way, you build a little more trust in yourself and reduce the impact of others' impatience on your well-being behind the wheel.

Surviving Freeways and Merging with Confidence

Freeways have a reputation for feeling like the pinnacle of driving anxiety—high speeds, constant merging, and the sense that you can't just "escape" whenever you want. If you find yourself white-knuckling the wheel at the thought of merging or dreading those big green overhead signs, you're part of a huge club. Many drivers, even those without anxiety, feel a spike in adrenaline right before an on-ramp. The key is breaking down what actually happens in those moments and turning chaos into a series of predictable, doable steps.

Let's start with the mechanics. Entering a freeway isn't about brute courage; it's about following a reliable sequence. As you approach the ramp, you want to gradually accelerate until you're matching the flow of traffic. This isn't the time to slam on the gas or crawl along—just find a steady, comfortable speed that lets you blend in. Signal early. While your blinker is on, check your mirrors, then tilt your head for a quick shoulder glance to spot any cars in your blind spots. The goal is to identify a gap that feels safe—don't rush or force it. When you see your opening, continue accelerating and merge smoothly, keeping your steering gentle and your eyes scanning forward. Once in the right lane, turn off your signal and settle into the flow.

When you're working up to freeway comfort, stick to the right lane. It's less intimidating, with slower speeds and easier access to exits. Plan your first practice drives so exits are frequent—maybe every mile or two—so you never feel boxed in. If possible, preview your route on a map and pick an entry point with a long on-ramp and wide shoulders. For some, just merging for one exit at a time is enough for a session; park at a rest stop or gas station afterward, breathe, and remind yourself that nothing catastrophic happened.

Mental cues can be lifesavers in high-speed environments. I often tell students to repeat, "Eyes forward, hands steady, one mile at a time." This anchor phrase keeps your attention on what matters—what's happening ahead of you—not what's behind or what other drivers are thinking. Fight the urge to fixate on your rearview mirror; instead, focus your gaze three to five seconds ahead of your car. Notice the car in front of you, watch for brake lights, and let the rest fade into background noise. This quick scan approach helps quiet nerves and keeps you grounded in reality.

Sometimes anxiety spikes right before or during a merge. That's normal. If you feel your breath tightening or your muscles clenching, try a micro-reset: take one deep breath in as you check your mirror, then slowly exhale as you glance over your shoulder. Imagine exhaling away some of that tension as you glide into your lane. If you miss your intended gap, don't panic—maintain speed and look for the next opening. There's no rule that says you must merge at a particular second; you have permission to wait for what feels safe.

Building freeway confidence is all about incremental exposure. One reader shared how she started with early Sunday mornings when traffic was thin. The first week was just driving up the ramp and immediately taking the first exit. Over time, she added a second exit, then tried busier times of day. With practice, her body learned that merging didn't always mean panic or disaster— her confidence grew as her anxiety shrank. Another driver found it helpful to record audio encouragements on his phone: short messages like "You've done this before," or "Take it slow—no rush." He played these before merging for reassurance, making his own voice a source of comfort.

If you run into trouble mid-drive—maybe traffic suddenly thickens, or someone cuts you off—remind yourself that exits are always coming up. You can leave the freeway at any point to regroup, and there's no shame in doing so. Sometimes just knowing that you have an "escape hatch" makes it easier to stay calm for longer stretches.

Visual: Safe Merging Checklist

- Accelerate to match speed with traffic
- Signal early (at least 3–5 seconds before merging)
- Check mirrors and blind spots with a quick shoulder glance
- Find a safe gap and merge smoothly
- Settle into the right lane
- Plan frequent exit options along your route

Every successful merge—even if it's only one exit—counts as progress. The more you break down freeway driving into manageable parts and practice each piece, the more those huge highways start to look like just another road you can handle. Confidence doesn't show up all at once; it grows each time you prove to yourself that you can merge, adjust, and keep going—even with nerves riding shotgun.

Parking Lot Anxiety: Strategies for Tight Spaces and Crowds

It's wild how a simple errand can feel like an obstacle course before you even step inside the store. Tight parking lots, crowded rows, cars circling like sharks—your pulse quickens just pulling in. Maybe you've felt your mind racing as you squeezed through a narrow lane, other drivers close behind, eyes darting for any open space. You might have left plenty of time for your trip, only to find yourself circling again and again for a spot that feels safe enough. That unease is real. For lots of adults who deal with driving anxiety, parking lots are where nerves spike the hardest.

Before entering a busy lot, it helps to run through a pre-parking routine built around your comfort. First, slow down at the entrance and circle once, letting yourself get the lay of the land. Don't rush—let others zip past if they want. Seek out end spots or spaces near exits. These usually give more room for opening doors and make leaving less stressful. If you're worried about being boxed in, consider backing into a spot so exiting later feels easier—you'll have a clear view and won't need to reverse into traffic. Many anxious drivers prefer spots near the store entrance or beside islands, fences, or curbs because there's only one car next to you instead of two. If it feels helpful, sketch a quick map of your usual shopping lot on paper or in your mind and mark "safest" zones—the ones that feel open, visible, and easy to maneuver in and out of. You'll find that just having a plan makes a crowded lot more tolerable.

Pressure from other drivers can turn parking into a high-stakes moment. The urge to hurry or park perfectly while someone waits behind you can be intense. But you get to set the pace. Use this internal script: "It's okay to take my time and let others go around me." Signal your intention early—flip on your blinker well before you start turning. If someone honks or gestures impatiently, keep your eyes forward and focus on your own process. Most drivers are in their own heads; they'll forget about you the moment they find their own spot. The truth is, nearly everyone has struggled with parking at some point—they just don't talk about it.

When parking feels overwhelming, visualization can retrain your mind to expect calm instead of chaos. Try this exercise: before you get in the car, close your eyes and picture yourself pulling into an empty lot. See yourself choosing a wide-open space, steering smoothly, parking straight, and stepping out relaxed. Imagine repeating this with one or two cars nearby next time. Over several sessions, build up to parking in a nearly full row, always picturing yourself breathing steadily through each step. Practice during off-peak hours first—a Sunday night or Tuesday morning—when most spaces are empty and there's no crowd. Once you feel more at ease, add a few more cars each time or visit when it's a little busier. Progress is personal; what matters is steady improvement rather than speed.

Some people find confidence grows faster with support. One reader wrote about how she'd avoided grocery shopping for months because the lot made her panic. She started by driving to empty lots after hours, just practicing pulling in and out of spots with no audience and no pressure. Over time, she'd park closer to the main entrance or try when there were scattered cars around. Another new driver teamed up with a "parking buddy"—her sister— who'd sit beside her for the first attempts during busier times. The buddy kept conversation light, reminded her to breathe, and never rushed her through the process. After a few weeks, she could park solo even when the lot was busy.

Handling tight spaces and crowds doesn't require perfection or bravado; it's about building predictable routines and practicing until anxiety fades into background noise. Remember that every small effort counts—you're rewriting old patterns and giving yourself permission to take up space, literally and figuratively. Your parking spot doesn't have to be the closest or fanciest; it just needs to work for you. And if you need an extra lap to find it, that's not failing—that's self-respect in action.

Night Driving and Bad Weather: Staying Calm in Unfamiliar Conditions

Night and bad-weather driving can unsettle even skilled drivers. Dark roads, glaring headlights, and pounding rain ramp up anxiety, with worries about missing a turn, not spotting hazards, or losing traction on slick surfaces. Many people avoid driving in these conditions altogether, but with preparation and gradual exposure, managing night and stormy drives can become less stressful. Here's how to build confidence and control before you hit the road.

Start by preparing your car. Reduced visibility makes prep essential. Check headlights for clarity and function—wipe off any grime. Test windshield wipers and replace them if they streak or skip. Check tire pressure; good tires grip better on wet or icy roads. Ensure you have enough gas so you're not scrambling for a station late at night or during a storm. Plan your route ahead, favoring familiar, well-lit roads and avoiding construction or winding back routes. Keep an emergency kit in your car with a flashlight, phone charger, water, snack, and a blanket or towel—you'll appreciate this if you get stuck or need to wait for help in rough conditions.

Gradual exposure works for driving at night and in bad weather. Build comfort slowly rather than jumping in all at once. If night driving makes you anxious, begin with short trips at dusk as streetlights come on—this helps your eyes adjust while you get used to the changing light. Once dusk feels manageable, try a familiar route after dark, like a drive to a nearby grocery store. Extend your trips gradually only after gaining comfort with shorter, known routes.

Apply the same approach to stormy weather. If rain intimidates you, test the waters during a light drizzle. Bring a supportive friend for early practice— someone calming who can reassure you through nervous moments. Once you're comfortable, work up to heavier rain or fog. Snow and ice call for extra caution and are best tackled only after you've gotten used to milder challenges.

Anxiety spikes when visibility drops and your mind starts predicting disaster. Prepared scripts can help steady your nerves: repeat to yourself, "Reduced visibility means everyone is moving slower. I'm allowed to take my time." Or, "If conditions feel unsafe, I can always pull over." These reminders help interrupt anxious thoughts and direct your focus to what's under your control.

Many have overcome night and bad-weather driving fears by practicing in small, structured steps. One person who panicked at dark highway exits started with neighborhood drives just after sunset and only expanded her comfort zone after repeated success. Another, nervous about rain after a previous skid, began as a passenger in light showers, then drove short distances with a supportive friend. With consistent, gradual exposure, once-daunting drives became routine.

The key to calm is familiarity. Every small, planned outing shows your brain that the drive will likely end safely, reinforcing resilience and reducing fear over time.

Ultimately, success with night and bad-weather driving depends on preparation and patience. You can't control darkness or rain, but you can control your readiness and the pace at which you challenge yourself. Each small, prepared drive builds self-trust.

Reflection: Night & Weather Confidence Log

After each low-visibility or bad-weather drive, quickly record where you went, what the conditions were, something that went well, and any anxious moments that you handled. Periodically reviewing these notes reveals patterns and solid proof of your progress—showing that steadfast effort does lessen anxiety.

Night streets and stormy skies may never be your favorite, but they don't have to keep you home. With preparation and kind self-talk, these drives become part of everyday life behind the wheel.

As we wrap up this chapter on common triggers, remember: each challenge you face makes the next less daunting. Up next, we'll cover tracking your progress and bouncing back from setbacks—helping you keep moving forward with confidence, no matter the road ahead.

11

Chapter 8: Seeking Support and Communicating Your Needs

Scripts for Talking About Your Anxiety with Family and Friends

The truth is, many people carry their driving anxiety in silence, worried about being misunderstood or dismissed. You might have sat through family dinners, listening to others swap road trip stories, all the while feeling that tightness in your chest. Maybe you've said "I'm just tired" or "The traffic is too much today" when you really meant "I can't face the wheel right now." The hardest part sometimes isn't the fear itself, but the loneliness that tags along with it. It's easy to imagine loved ones won't get it, or that they'll think it isn't a real problem. But keeping your struggle hidden only makes that burden heavier. Breaking that silence—bringing someone else into your experience—isn't easy, but it can be a powerful step toward relief.

Opening up to someone about your driving anxiety doesn't require a dramatic confession. A simple, direct statement can set the stage for real understanding. If you're not sure where to start, try this: "I've been struggling with driving anxiety, and I want to let you know because your support matters to me." It's honest and clear. You're not asking for a fix or an immediate solution—you're letting someone in on what's real for you. You might add, "Sometimes, I need to go at my own pace or change plans last minute—thank you for understanding." This lets your friend or family member know that flexibility and patience are part of what will help you most.

It's natural to worry that others might minimize your struggle or brush it aside with "everyone gets nervous driving sometimes" or "just get over it." When that happens, it can sting. It's tempting to shrink back, but there's power in calmly setting the record straight. You might say, "I know it might seem small, but this is a big deal for me. I appreciate you listening." This invites empathy without demanding it and plants a seed for future conversations. If shame creeps in—as it does for many—remind yourself that honesty is not weakness. You can say, "It's not always easy to talk about, but I want to be honest so you're not left guessing." That kind of openness can take some of the pressure off both you and your loved ones.

Sometimes what helps most is naming specific needs or boundaries. You're allowed to ask for exactly what will make things easier for you. If you're anxious about having a passenger, or worried about letting someone down if plans change, spell it out: "If I say I need to pull over or take a break, please just give me some space and encouragement." Or, if unsolicited advice makes you feel overwhelmed, try: "I'm working on this at my own pace and may not want advice unless I ask for it." People often jump to fix things because they care—but sometimes solutions create more stress than support. Letting them know what helps makes things smoother for everyone.

Encouragement is a double-edged sword. Sometimes a well-meaning "You can do it!" feels like extra pressure instead of comfort. It's okay to tell people how and when you want encouragement: "Sometimes encouragement helps, but sometimes it just adds pressure—I'll let you know what I need in the moment." This gives you control and keeps communication clear.

It's one thing to read scripts; it's another to see how these conversations actually play out in real life. I remember working with a student named Mia who dreaded telling her partner about her driving anxiety. She'd been making excuses for months—avoiding joint errands and family outings—until she finally blurted out, "Driving freaks me out and I don't know what to do anymore." Her partner didn't laugh or brush her off. Instead, he listened and started helping with grocery runs, taking turns behind the wheel without making her feel guilty. Mia told me later she felt immediate relief—not because her fear vanished, but because she was no longer hiding.

Another story that sticks with me comes from a small group of friends who'd always shared rides to work events and weekend outings. When one of them admitted she was struggling with highway driving, instead of teasing her or leaving her out, they coordinated errands together. Sometimes they'd offer to carpool or pick up groceries; other times they'd just keep her company on short drives so she didn't feel so alone. It shifted the vibe from pressure to partnership, and that trust made all the difference.

Interactive Reflection: Your Conversation Blueprint

Take a few minutes to write down answers to these questions before your next talk about driving anxiety:

- Who do you trust most to start this conversation with?
- What's one specific thing you wish they understood about your experience?
- Which script above feels most natural for your voice? If none do, how would you say it in your own words?
- What's one boundary or request you want to make clear (e.g., "Please don't give advice unless I ask")?
- How will you know the conversation went well? What does support look like for you?

Jotting these down can help organize your thoughts and make the actual conversation less daunting. Keep your notes handy—as a cheat sheet if nerves hit, or as a reminder that your needs matter just as much as anyone else's.

Opening up about driving anxiety isn't just about getting help—it's about building bridges back to connection and trust with the people around you. Even if the first conversation feels awkward or imperfect, each step chips away at isolation and shame. Often, people respond better than we expect when given a chance to understand what we're going through. Even if they don't get it right away, being honest clears up confusion and makes space for new kinds of support.

When and How to Involve a Professional

Sometimes, the weight of driving anxiety just doesn't lift, no matter how many strategies you try on your own. If you find yourself stuck in a cycle of panic, or if your fear keeps you from living the life you want—missing appointments, skipping out on family gatherings, or turning down work opportunities—then it's time to think about getting extra help. You might notice that you avoid driving altogether, or maybe you get behind the wheel but are overwhelmed by intense dread every single time. For some, the symptoms are physical: racing heart, shaky hands, even full-blown panic attacks that leave you breathless or dizzy. Others find their world shrinking as they plan their days to avoid highways, bridges, or even short trips to the store. If you recognize yourself in any of these patterns, especially if they have lasted weeks or months, it's a sign that reaching out to a professional could make a real difference.

There's no shame in seeking help when driving anxiety doesn't budge. In fact, some of the strongest people I've met are those who've said, "I can't do this alone anymore." If you're not sure whether it's time to involve a professional, it helps to look for a few telltale signs. Start with a quick checklist: Are you having persistent panic attacks when you drive? Has your avoidance started to interfere with work, relationships, or daily activities? Have you tried self-help strategies for weeks with little or no improvement? Do you feel severe distress at the idea of even getting in the car? If you answered "yes" to any of these, especially more than one, it's probably time to look for outside support.

Finding the right therapist or clinician can sound intimidating at first, but it gets easier once you know what to look for. The best place to start is with an online directory that lets you filter providers by specialty. Sites like Psychology Today and the Anxiety and Depression Association of America offer search tools where you can enter keywords like "anxiety," "CBT" (Cognitive Behavioral Therapy), or "phobias." This narrows down your options to people with training in exactly what you're facing. Take time to read provider profiles—look for mentions of exposure therapy, trauma-informed care, or experience working with driving fears. You might also call your primary care doctor for recommendations. Don't be afraid to send a brief email or leave a voicemail asking about their experience with driving anxiety; a good therapist will understand that finding the right fit is important.

If you've never started this kind of conversation before, it helps to have a few short scripts ready for reaching out. You could say to your doctor or provider, "I'm experiencing intense anxiety when I drive, and it's impacting my life—can you help or refer me?" This gets straight to the point and signals that your concern is serious. Or if you prefer being more direct about your needs: "I'd like to explore therapy for my driving anxiety. Do you have recommendations?" These openers take the pressure off—you don't need to have all the answers right away. Your provider should take your concerns seriously and help connect you with someone who can offer targeted support.

Walking into therapy for the first time can feel like stepping into unknown territory. Many people picture awkward silences or endless digging into their childhoods, but modern therapy is usually much more collaborative and practical. During your first session, expect to answer intake questions about your symptoms, daily life, and what brought you in. Your therapist will want to know how anxiety shows up for you—when it started, how often it happens, what triggers it, and what (if anything) helps. This isn't about judgment; it's about building a clear picture so they can tailor strategies specifically for you. You'll work together to set goals—maybe being able to drive solo on local roads or handling highway traffic without panic. Confidentiality is standard; what you share stays private, except in rare cases involving safety.

If Cognitive Behavioral Therapy (CBT) comes up—and it often does for phobias and anxiety—it means you'll be working on shifting unhelpful thought patterns and gradually practicing feared situations in small steps. Exposure therapy is a subset of CBT where you systematically face anxious triggers with professional guidance and support until they lose their power over you.

It's normal to worry that therapy will be uncomfortable at times. Facing fears isn't always pleasant—sometimes it means sitting with anxiety until it fades rather than running from it—but a good therapist will go at your pace and celebrate every milestone right alongside you. Progress isn't always dramatic; sometimes it shows up as being able to drive one extra block before turning back or feeling only mildly uneasy instead of terrified on a familiar route. Some readers have found that just knowing they have an expert in their corner changes everything—the fear feels less overwhelming when shared.

A medical consultation can also be an option if anxiety is severe or accompanied by depression or other health issues. Doctors sometimes suggest medication as a temporary tool while you build coping skills in therapy. If medication is recommended, it should be part of a broader plan that includes learning practical strategies—not a stand-alone fix.

Above all, remember that needing professional help doesn't mean you've failed or that your anxiety is too big to solve. It simply means your brain and body need extra support right now—and there are people trained and ready to provide it. Taking this step is not giving up control; it's reclaiming it in a new way—one guided by expertise and compassion rather than fear.

Joining Peer Support Groups—Online and In Person

There's something powerful about realizing you're not the only one dreading a steering wheel or tensing up at intersections. Driving anxiety can feel isolating, but connecting with others who understand replaces shame with recognition, empathy, and even shared laughter. Peer support groups give you a space where your struggles are validated instead of dismissed, and where small wins—like handling a red light calmly—are celebrated.

The benefits go beyond being understood. These groups are full of practical tips that stick because they come from people who've lived through the same challenges. You might discover a podcast that makes traffic tolerable, a breathing technique that worked for someone else, or encouragement that feels more real than "You'll be fine." Hearing, "I remember that fear—here's what helped me," can be a game-changer.

Finding a group is easier than you may think. Online options include Facebook communities, Reddit forums, or virtual meetups hosted by national organizations. If you prefer in person, check Meetup.com, local hospitals, or behavioral health clinics. Each group has its own style—some busy and global, others small and intimate—so explore until you find the right fit.

When joining, keep etiquette simple: respect privacy, listen actively, and remember everyone is at a different stage. Share your main challenge and one goal if you're comfortable, but know that just listening at first is perfectly fine. Over time, you'll likely feel ready to contribute encouragement or share what's worked for you.

It's natural to feel nervous about opening up. Start small—respond to a post with "I can relate," or quietly attend a meeting without sharing. Comfort builds with time, and engagement at your own pace is what matters most.

Peer support can be transformative. One reader found an accountability partner online, checking in before practice drives and cheering each other's progress. Another nervously attended a local group and left with new friends and tips that gave him hope. Simply showing up—whether online or in person—is itself an act of courage. In these spaces, anxiety doesn't isolate you; it connects you to people who want to see you succeed.

Teaching Your Support Person to Help—Without Taking Over

Driving with someone you trust can be a comfort, but their behavior can either calm your nerves or make anxiety worse. A steady, patient presence helps; nagging, criticism, or taking control fuels fear. Most loved ones mean well but don't always know what helps, which is why an upfront conversation makes all the difference.

Be clear about your needs. Calm silence, patient listening, and gentle encouragement ("You're doing fine") are supportive. In contrast, pushing you to take highways or criticizing mistakes almost always backfires. A short "training chat" before driving together can set expectations. For example: "If

I get anxious, please remind me to use my breathing technique—not just to relax." Small changes in wording can shift the mood completely.

You can even share a simple guide:

Support Person Do's:

- Stay calm, even if I'm nervous
- Ask if I want to talk or prefer quiet
- Offer gentle encouragement when needed
- Respect my choice to pause or pull over

Support Person Don'ts:

- Don't grab the wheel unless there's real danger
- Don't shout instructions or criticize mistakes
- Don't push me past my comfort zone

A safe word or signal, like tapping the dashboard, can also help—letting you ask for quiet or a break without explaining mid-drive.

Even with the best intentions, tension may rise. If support starts to feel like pressure, pause or practice alone for a while. After drives, talk honestly: "When you told me to merge faster, I lost focus," or, "When you stayed quiet, it helped." These check-ins build trust and reduce frustration.

Support partnerships thrive when both sides adapt. One sibling pair agreed on "gentle co-piloting," where help was offered only if asked—turning stressful outings into shared victories. Another driver used the checklist with her spouse, which removed guesswork and created a calmer atmosphere.

When done right, a supportive partner not only cheers your progress but makes the journey less lonely. Teaching your support person how to help is about more than driving—it's about building respect, trust, and teamwork. Setting boundaries isn't weakness; it's what allows both of you to move forward with confidence, one mile at a time.

The next chapter will cover how to sustain these gains in the long run—so that your confidence sticks with you for the journey ahead.

12

Chapter 9: Sustaining Success and Enjoying Freedom

Preventing Relapse: Staying Resilient After Success

Imagine pulling into your driveway after a drive you once thought impossible. That old tension in your shoulders has faded, and you feel proud. You've gained freedom and might even enjoy driving now. Then, suddenly, anxiety creeps back one morning, or you avoid a route you'd previously conquered. It's confusing—you might wonder if you're back to square one or if all your progress was lost. This is where resilience matters most.

Progress with driving anxiety is rarely a straight line. Temporary setbacks— like feeling anxious on an unfamiliar road or during a tough week—don't erase your gains. Think of these moments as stumbles on a hike; they aren't cliffs but small bumps along the path. For example, if your heart pounds or your hands tighten on a new stretch of highway, the difference now is you remember your grounding and breathing exercises. Even pulling over for a minute is not failure, but using your hard-won skills to stay safe and steady.

The distinction between a setback and a relapse lies in persistence and perspective. Setbacks are tough days or weeks, when the nerves return but you still keep driving, even if you temporarily take it slower or stick to easier routes.

A relapse, however, is slipping back into persistent avoidance—canceling plans, skipping drives for weeks, or feeling hopeless. Most people with driving anxiety face the occasional setback. It's human. What matters is not allowing these episodes to erase recognition of your progress.

To stay resilient, stick to a routine. Just as muscles need regular use, your driving confidence requires gentle, regular maintenance. Schedule low-pressure drives—maybe Sunday morning coffee runs or afternoon trips to the park. Keep these outings in your routine even when you feel confident. It's easy to think, "I don't need this anymore," but confidence fades if unused. Those short, regular drives can keep anxiety at bay and prevent doubts from creeping in.

Every month, review your progress tracker or gratitude journal. Look at notes about challenges you've faced and overcome. Notice how formerly scary routes no longer intimidate you or how quickly you bounce back from anxiety compared to six months ago. This isn't just feel-good fluff—it shifts your brain's expectations toward success over setbacks. Sometimes you'll realize you handled a challenge instinctively, proving your skills have become second nature.

Despite this, life inevitably throws curveballs. New situations—a move, a job change, even switching doctors—can revive old fears. Health setbacks or changing seasons, like dark winter mornings or sudden summer storms, can also shake your confidence as driving feels less familiar. These transitions challenge everyone, but for those working through driving anxiety, they can be especially unsettling.

When these triggers appear, early intervention is key. The faster you notice the signs—avoiding routes, making excuses, or feeling dread before a drive—the easier it is to steer back on course. Ask yourself, "I've noticed some old fears coming back. What's one small step I can take today?" This might mean returning to an easier route, re-practicing breathing techniques, or reaching out to a supportive friend.

Early Warning Checklist: Is It Time to Revisit Exposure Steps?

- Are you avoiding routes that used to feel routine?
- Is anxiety rising before drives?
- Are you finding excuses to skip outings?
- Has your confidence dropped after a stressful event?
- Are you needing more reassurance than usual?

If you answer "yes" to two or more, it's a good idea to revisit your exposure hierarchy—the step-by-step plan you used before. Start by repeating a step that now feels only mildly uncomfortable. Remember, you've succeeded at this before, and you still possess those skills.

Having proactive strategies ready helps too. Some people schedule "check-in drives" each month—drives with no pressure and no destination besides keeping your skills sharp. Others keep their gratitude journal in sight, as a reminder of what they've overcome and why they persist.

Relapse prevention isn't about eliminating anxiety forever. It's about catching small setbacks before they grow and using the tools you know are effective (A Healthy Push, n.d.; Headspace, n.d.). The most resilient drivers aren't anxiety-free—they simply keep showing up, treating setbacks as signals to use their strategies, not as reasons to stop.

Creating a simple "relapse plan" can help. Write down the three tools that help most when anxiety returns—perhaps mindful breathing, calling a friend, or reviewing your progress—and keep them handy in your car or phone notes. This way, when anxiety resurfaces, you don't have to rely on memory; you can just follow your own advice.

You've already proven that growth is real—setbacks don't define you. Your progress is lasting because it's rooted in practice, patience, and kindness to yourself, not perfection. When life changes or anxieties resurface, know your tools and strength remain.

Driving as Self-Care: Turning Routine Drives into Confidence Boosters

There's something powerful about sitting behind the wheel and realizing you're not just getting from place to place—you're taking care of yourself. For a long time, driving might have felt like a test, a threat, even a punishment. But what if you began to treat driving as an act of self-care? Not just a chore, but a moment carved out for your own growth and self-respect. Imagine choosing to take the long scenic route on a sunny afternoon, not because it's faster or easier, but because you want to enjoy the view, listen to your favorite playlist, and move at your own pace. There's value in reclaiming this everyday activity as something that supports your well-being. Each time you drive by choice, you reinforce your independence, and that alone is worth celebrating.

Shifting your mindset starts with intention. Instead of rushing to finish errands or dreading the drive to work, try pairing your routine drives with simple pleasures that speak to you. Maybe you've got a podcast that always makes you laugh or a playlist that boosts your mood, so you make it a ritual to press play the moment you buckle up. Some days, calling a supportive friend (on hands-free, of course) while you're heading home can turn a regular drive into an uplifting check-in. These rituals don't just distract from anxiety—they infuse your driving with positive associations and remind you that you're in control. Over time, the car becomes less a cage and more a comfort zone.

Errands and short drives can be reframed as mini-victories. Picking up groceries or mailing a letter—mundane tasks for many—become small chances to flex your growing confidence. Each successful trip is tangible proof that anxiety doesn't get the final say. If you're feeling ambitious, challenge yourself with tiny goals: park in a busy lot and stay calm, try out a new route, or drive during a slightly busier time of day. When you come back without panic and with the groceries in hand, pause for a second and let that win sink in.

There's also something special about using these everyday successes as fuel for growth in other parts of life. Ask yourself: if I could move from white-knuckling every drive to choosing routes with curiosity and even joy, what else am I capable of? Maybe driving to a new part of town opens the door to trying out a pottery class or joining an evening book club. Perhaps the confidence gained behind the wheel spills into public speaking at work or saying "yes" to a spontaneous road trip with friends. You start to see how conquering one fear has ripple effects across your life.

Reader stories make these ideas real and relatable. One woman told me how she used to dread grocery runs, but after practicing her coping tools and sticking with short trips, she noticed something shift. She started looking forward to these weekly drives, treating them like "me time" to unwind with her favorite songs and reflect on her progress. The grocery store stopped being just another battleground and became a place where she could notice how far she'd come. That simple shift—finding gratitude in the ordinary—gave her confidence not just as a driver but as someone who could handle whatever came her way.

I invite you to take a moment and think about a recent drive that went well, or even just felt less stressful than usual. Maybe it was the drive home after work where you realized halfway through that your hands weren't gripping the wheel so tightly, or an afternoon when traffic didn't bother you as much as it once did. What made this drive different? Was it your favorite music, a new mindset, or simply the fact that you kept going even when nerves kicked in? Jot down those details in your journal or phone notes. These reflections aren't just nice memories—they're blueprints for future success.

Here's a little exercise if you're looking for inspiration: next week, pick one drive you usually see as routine—a school run, pharmacy stop, or coffee pickup—and approach it as an opportunity for self-care. Before getting in the car, set an intention for how you want to feel or what you want to notice on the drive. Decide on one uplifting ritual for the ride—maybe it's listening to an audiobook, reciting an affirmation when stopped at red lights, or simply enjoying the quiet if that feels restful. Afterward, reflect on how the experience felt compared to your usual drives.

As your comfort grows, consider expanding your horizons. Plan outings that aren't just about necessity but about pleasure—a drive through the countryside to see wildflowers in bloom, an evening spin around town with windows down and music up, or even just exploring new neighborhoods at your own pace. These moments don't have to be grand; even small adventures can plant seeds of freedom and possibility.

Driving can transform from something you dread into an act of self-respect and joy. When you approach each drive as a form of self-care—pairing it with practices that make you feel grounded, proud, or connected—you're not just reinforcing your independence behind the wheel; you're reminding yourself that growth is possible in every part of your life.

Interactive Reflection Prompt

Think back on the last month. Describe one drive that felt easy or even enjoyable. What contributed to that feeling? Was it something you did differently, a shift in attitude, or just having more trust in yourself? Write about it briefly—capture the details while they're fresh. If possible, share this reflection with someone supportive or keep it somewhere visible as a reminder of how far you've come.

Adapting Strategies for Life Changes and New Challenges

Life never sits still. Just when you start to feel steady, something shifts—a new car, a move, a change in family roles—and suddenly, the road feels unfamiliar again. If you've lived with driving anxiety, you know how change can make old nerves pop up in strange new ways. The good news is, you're not starting over from scratch. The strength and skills you've built travel with you, but sometimes they need an update for your new reality.

Picture this: you finally feel comfortable in your compact sedan, every button and blind spot memorized, only to upgrade to a bigger SUV. The first time you slide behind the wheel, it feels like driving a barge through narrow streets. Everything from the turning radius to the dash controls is different. Your hands sweat, and you notice yourself hesitating at parking lots you used to breeze through. In moments like these, flexibility becomes your best friend. Rather than expecting instant comfort, give yourself permission to treat this as an unfamiliar skill. Go back to basics—practice parking maneuvers in empty lots, adjust your mirrors with care, and spend time sitting in the car just getting used to the new sights and sounds. Your exposure ladder can easily be adapted for "new car" steps: start with stationary time, then short drives on quiet roads, building up to trickier scenarios. Each repeat builds muscle memory, and soon enough, what felt alien becomes routine.

Moving to a new city brings its own set of hurdles. Suddenly, the streets are crowded with buses and cyclists, or maybe public transit is now part of your daily commute. Weather might throw you a curveball: rainstorms if you're used to sun, or snow after years in a mild climate. It's normal to feel a surge of worry as you face traffic patterns or weather conditions outside your comfort zone. Here, ongoing self-assessment is key. Listen for anxiety signals—tension before drives, hesitancy with new routes—and don't ignore them. Instead of letting overwhelm take over, break things into manageable chunks. For heavy city traffic, design a "city driving" exposure plan. Start by observing as a passenger on public transit or ride along with a friend. Next, try short trips at off-peak hours, gradually layering in more complexity as your confidence grows. If weather is your main concern, practice in safe conditions first—a light drizzle before a downpour, or dusk before full darkness—and use support tools like weather apps or traffic cameras to build predictability into your routine.

Sometimes the challenge isn't the environment but the people depending on you. Becoming a caregiver or parent often means driving with children or vulnerable adults in the car. The pressure doubles: not only are you responsible for yourself, but also for someone who may need your attention mid-drive. This can spike anxiety even for seasoned drivers. Preparation is everything here. Set up car seats and supplies well before leaving so you're not fumbling at the last minute. Do practice runs alone or with another adult first if possible. Try short drives around the block with your passenger before tackling longer outings. If possible, create backup plans—a friend who can be called for help, or safe spots to pull over if you need a break. Remember: needing to pause and regroup is a sign of wisdom, not weakness.

As life shifts, revisit your exposure hierarchy often. Exposure ladders aren't static—they should evolve with your needs and challenges. Let's say you now work night shifts and find yourself anxious about dark roads and empty highways. Draft a new exposure plan: begin by standing outside at night to get used to darkness, sit in your car under streetlights without driving, then practice short drives on well-lit streets before building up to longer commutes at off-hours. Adjust each step's difficulty based on your real-time anxiety level—not what you think you "should" be able to handle.

Transitions often disrupt established routines and coping strategies, so troubleshooting is part of the process. When things get shaken up—new car, job schedule changes, or a move—build in extra practice time for adjustment. This isn't wasted effort; it's preventative maintenance for your confidence. Even a few extra laps around familiar blocks or extra sessions practicing parallel parking help anchor your skills in the face of change.

Support is crucial during big transitions. If you feel stuck or find anxiety creeping back in after a major life event, reach out for help early instead of toughing it out alone. Sometimes a single refresher session with a driving instructor can clear up uncertainties about a new vehicle or local traffic rules. Local support groups (in person or online) often have members facing similar challenges—don't hesitate to ask for advice about tackling city congestion or navigating winter roads.

Treating change as an opportunity rather than a threat transforms your mindset over time. Each new challenge is proof that your resilience grows as you adapt. One reader shared how she moved from southern California's sunshine to Minnesota's snowy winters after retirement. She started small—practicing on empty side streets after snowfalls, learning how her car handled on ice, and building up to busier roads only when she felt steady again. It took patience and plenty of self-kindness, but now she laughs that she's the one giving winter driving tips to her neighbors.

Whenever life hands you something new behind the wheel—whether it's a different car, a busier cityscape, or family counting on your safe arrival— remind yourself: "Every new challenge is a chance to prove my resilience." Update your toolkit regularly. Trust that you already have everything you need inside you to adapt and succeed—even when the road looks different than before.

Celebrating Your Driving Independence—Your New Normal

It's easy to overlook how far you've come when you're focused on the next goal, but your ability to drive with confidence is no small victory. Remember those days when sitting in the car felt like a test of willpower? Maybe your hands shook, or your chest tightened at the thought of merging into traffic. Now, look at you: driving to work, visiting friends, or running errands without the suffocating weight of fear. That's not just a little progress—it's a transformation worth honoring. Many people never know how intense driving anxiety can feel, so only you can truly appreciate the courage it takes to keep showing up, practice after practice. This is your new normal—one built on hard work and persistence.

Take a moment to reflect on everything you've accomplished. The courage required to face your fears often goes unrecognized by others, but don't let it go unnoticed by you. One way to make this real is to write a letter to your past self. Picture yourself at the beginning—full of doubt, maybe even convinced you'd never drive again. What would you tell that version of you now? Describe the hurdles you've cleared, the skills you've built, and the life that opened up because you didn't give up. Writing this letter isn't just about making yourself feel good; it's a concrete reminder that change is possible, even when it once felt unreachable.

Some people find it powerful to create a visual record of their progress. You might collect photos or mementos from drives that once seemed impossible—a selfie in front of a landmark, a ticket from a favorite event, or even a map with routes you now travel with ease. Put these together in a collage or journal. Label one side "Before"—with words or images that captured the struggle—and the other "After," showing your victories and freedoms. When doubt creeps back in, flip through these pages and let them remind you of what's possible.

Milestones deserve real celebration. Maybe it's time for that outing you used to avoid—the beach at sunrise, a favorite restaurant across town, or a visit to see family you haven't hugged in too long. Plan this trip not as another exposure exercise, but as a reward for your persistence. Make it special: pack your favorite snacks, invite a supportive friend, or choose music that lifts your spirits. If a big trip feels daunting, start small. Even treating yourself to a meaningful token—a new keychain, a license plate frame with an empowering message, or a small trinket for your dashboard—can symbolize how far you've come. These aren't just trinkets; they're reminders of your strength.

The impact of your progress doesn't stop with you. Sharing your story can bring hope to others who feel stuck in their own fears. Maybe someone in your life is quietly struggling—mentioning your experience could open the door for honest conversation and support. If you feel comfortable, post a message in an online support group or submit a short story to a driving anxiety blog. Even just leaving a comment on someone else's post can spark encouragement and connection. You might be surprised by how many people reach out privately to thank you for saying what they couldn't put into words. Your experience has value—not just as personal proof of change, but as inspiration for the next person searching for hope.

Sometimes the most meaningful moments come from helping someone else along the path you once found so daunting. If you know someone facing their own driving fears, offer to listen without judgment or give gentle advice when asked. Share what helped you—whether it's breathing techniques, playlists, or simply patience with slow progress. The ripple effect of your courage can reach further than you imagine.

Now think about what lies ahead, free from the weight of constant dread. Picture yourself deciding on Saturday morning where you want to go—not where anxiety allows you to go—maybe taking spontaneous trips out of town or saying yes to last-minute invitations without hesitation. Imagine planning vacations where you drive rental cars along scenic highways or visiting new cities without worrying about unfamiliar streets. Visualize road trips with friends filled with laughter and music instead of tense silence and sweaty palms. These aren't just fantasies—they're real freedoms now within reach.

As you settle into this new relationship with driving, reflect on what new possibilities are opening up for you. Ask yourself: What adventures have I put off that now feel within reach? Who might I visit? What parts of my city or state are waiting for me to explore? Write down these new freedoms and keep them close as motivation for the days when anxiety tries to whisper old doubts.

Reflection Exercise

Sit down with a pen and paper—or open a blank note on your phone—and write a short letter to your past self about what you've accomplished behind the wheel. Don't hold back on the details, big or small. Describe what you once thought was impossible and how it feels now that it's real. You might also add a "before and after" photo collage or journal entry if visuals help make progress tangible.

In closing, give yourself credit for every single step along the way—the easy drives, the tough days, and everything in between. You've shifted from surviving each drive to truly living with freedom and choice. This isn't just about getting from point A to point B anymore; it's about reclaiming your independence and building a life that feels bigger and more possible than before.

As we move forward, keep this sense of pride close by—you've earned it. The road ahead is yours to explore, with confidence as your companion.

13

Conclusion

Take a slow, deep breath. You've made it to the end of the book, but honestly, this is just another beginning. Sitting here, reading these words, you've already done something brave. You chose to face your driving anxiety head-on. That's not easy. It takes guts to admit you want things to change, and even more courage to do the hard work of making it happen. I hope you let yourself feel proud—really proud—of every step you've taken, whether it was reading a chapter, practicing a breathing tool, or simply sitting behind the wheel with your heart pounding and choosing not to give up.

All along, I wanted this guide to feel like a steady hand on your shoulder. We started by honoring your unique story—your history, your triggers, the "what-ifs" that used to run wild before every drive. We explored the science of panic, not to scare you, but to make those body sensations less mysterious and less threatening. You learned to spot your patterns of avoidance and understand why they made sense, even if they kept you stuck. Naming shame, calling it out, and realizing you're not alone? That's not just information; that's relief.

From there, you built your own toolkit. You practiced pausing safely when panic hit, instead of powering through or beating yourself up. You learned the power of micro-achievements—those tiny wins that turn into real confidence, even if nobody else sees them. You tried breathing techniques, grounding exercises, and red light resets. You made panic pages and thought cards. Each tool is a small act of self-respect—a way to say, "I matter. My comfort matters."

You also took a hard look at the stories you tell yourself. You practiced new scripts, shifting from "I can't do this" to "I'm learning, and that's enough." You learned to reframe setbacks as data, not disaster. You tracked your progress, celebrated every sticker, badge, or note—even on the days that felt like a slog. That's resilience in action.

Practically, you've built routines and rituals that work for you. You set up your car for comfort, planned your routes, and found your own favorite playlist. You made peace with starting small: maybe just sitting in the car, driving the block, or circling a parking lot. Then, step by step, you moved into busier streets, learned to handle intersections and high-pressure moments, and even faced the big stuff—highways, bridges, tunnels, night driving, and bad weather. Sometimes with a shaky voice or trembling hands, but always with the determination to try again. That's how confidence is built—not in giant leaps, but in steady, stubborn practice.

Through it all, you learned that driving anxiety isn't a personal flaw. It's not a sign you're broken or unfit. It's a challenge—one that can be understood, managed, and gradually overcome. You found ways to ask for help, whether from family, friends, a therapist, or a support group. You learned to teach your supporters how to actually help, not just hover or criticize. You discovered that community—real, honest connection—can shrink shame and make the journey lighter.

The main pillars you've built on this road are real: self-understanding, daily mindset shifts, in-the-moment panic tools, thoughtful pre-drive routines, stepwise exposure, cognitive and mindfulness skills, troubleshooting strategies, progress tracking, seeking support, and growing lifelong resilience. These aren't just chapters—they're habits and mindsets you now own. You have options. You have agency. You have proof that you can do hard things, even when your brain tries to convince you otherwise.

The biggest takeaways? Progress is made of small, repeated actions, not giant leaps. Setbacks are normal and actually help you learn. Self-compassion is fuel—it gets you farther than any amount of grit or shame ever could. Personalization matters; this isn't a one-size-fits-all journey. Flexibility is your friend. And you never have to do this alone—help is out there, and you deserve it.

So, pause and celebrate. Remember the little wins: the first time you drove alone, said "no thanks" to an unhelpful suggestion, or parked in that tricky lot. Maybe you handled a tailgater without panicking, or took your first drive at dusk. These are not small things. They are signs that your world is expanding, one mile at a time.

I want you to see driving with new eyes now—as an act of self-care, a way to claim your independence, and a symbol of what's possible when you believe in your own growth. You own the road, not the other way around.

If you're wondering what's next, here it is: Pick one thing, just one, that feels doable today. Update your progress tracker. Plan a new route. Tell a friend how far you've come. Reach out for support if you need it. Maybe you offer encouragement to someone else still struggling—your story could be the nudge they need to try again. Recovery is ongoing. It bends, it shifts, it adapts to life changes. Keep checking in with yourself. Revisit your goals, your exposure ladder, and your favorite coping tools as your world—and your confidence—grow.

From me to you, thank you for trusting me with your story. I know how much courage it takes to ask for change, and I am genuinely honored to walk this road with you. Every reader who picks up this book is proof that hope and bravery are alive and well. I am cheering for you, always.

And if you ever doubt yourself, remember: You've already done the hardest thing—you started. That's how every journey to freedom begins. Keep going. The road is waiting, and you are ready. And who knows? Your story might be the light that guides someone else out of the dark.

A Note from the Author

Thank you for taking the time to read this book. I hope the strategies and stories inside have given you encouragement, practical tools, and a sense of support as you continue your journey toward calmer, more confident driving.

If you found this book helpful, would you consider leaving a review? Reviews not only help other readers discover resources that might benefit them, but they also give me valuable feedback to keep improving future guides.

Your voice matters—whether it's a few words about what you learned, or how the book made you feel, every review makes a difference.

Thank you again for being part of this journey. Drive safely, and take each step with patience and confidence.

References

- *What is driving anxiety? Causes, symptoms, and treatment* https://www.medicalnewstoday.com/articles/driving-anxiety
- *Panic attacks and panic disorder - Symptoms and causes* https://www.mayoclinic.org/diseases-conditions/panic-attacks/symptoms-causes/syc-20376021
- *The Trap of Avoidance and Safety Behaviors* https://www.psychologytoday.com/us/blog/anxiety-relief-for-kids-and-teens/202305/the-trap-of-avoidance-and-safety-behaviors
- *Anxiety Success Stories - Emily's Journey to Overcoming ...* https://www.ahealthypush.com/post/anxiety-success-stories-emily-s-journey-to-overcoming-driving-anxiety
- *Treating patients with driving phobia by virtual reality ...* https://pmc.ncbi.nlm.nih.gov/articles/PMC6946146/
- *Driving Anxiety: Overview, Causes, And How To Get Over It* https://healthmatch.io/anxiety/how-to-get-over-driving-anxiety
- *From Small Steps to Big Wins: The Importance of Celebrating* https://www.psychologytoday.com/us/blog/empower-your-mind/202406/from-small-steps-to-big-wins-the-importance-of-celebrating
- *How to Practice Self-Compassion: 8 Techniques and Tips* https://positivepsychology.com/how-to-practice-self-compassion/
- *What To Do During a Traffic Stop Procedure - Sloan Law Office* https://sloanlawkc.com/blog/what-to-do-during-a-traffic-stop-procedure/
- *Breathwork Interventions for Adults with Clinically ...* https://pmc.ncbi.nlm.nih.gov/articles/PMC9954474/
- *How to Manage a Panic Attack While Driving?* https://amfmtreatment.com/blog/how-to-manage-a-panic-attack-while-driving/

- *Building Your Driving Anxiety Toolkit: Practical Strategies ...* https://drivingtoindependence.com/driving-anxiety-toolkit-strategies-for-confident-drive/
- *Visualisation: A Powerful Tool for Overcoming Driving Anxiety* https://www.thedrivinganxietycoach.co.uk/visualisation-a-powerful-tool-for-overcoming-driving-anxiety/
- *How to Overcome Fear of Driving | Via* https://mwg.aaa.com/via/car/how-to-overcome-fear-driving
- *World's Most Relaxing Song May Reduce Anxiety by 65%* https://www.psychiatrist.com/news/worlds-most-relaxing-song-may-reduce-anxiety-by-65/
- *Self-Test for Anxiety* https://healthy.kaiserpermanente.org/health-wellness/health-encyclopedia/he.self-test-for-anxiety.abn2339
- *Driving Phobia* https://anxietycare.org.uk/phobias/driving-phobia/
- *Creating an Exposure Hierarchy | Article* https://www.therapistaid.com/therapy-guide/creating-an-exposure-hierarchy-guide
- *Can I apply mindfulness to driving?* https://www.headspace.com/articles/applying-mindfulness-to-driving
- *Anxiety Success Stories - Emily's Journey to Overcoming ...* https://www.ahealthypush.com/post/anxiety-success-stories-emily-s-journey-to-overcoming-driving-anxiety
- *Understanding the Fear of Driving – and How to Overcome It* https://manhattancbt.com/fear-driving/
- *Can I apply mindfulness to driving?* https://www.headspace.com/articles/applying-mindfulness-to-driving
- *30 Grounding Techniques to Quiet Distressing Thoughts* https://www.healthline.com/health/grounding-techniques
- *Using Coping Cards in Therapy: 13 Examples & Templates* https://positivepsychology.com/coping-cards/
- *Rush Hour Rage: How to Keep Calm and Avoid Accidents ...* https://www.becauseyouwanttowin.com/rush-hour-rage-how-to-keep-calm-and-avoid-accidents-in-heavy-traffic-in-georgia/
- *How to Deal with Tailgaters* https://www.progressive.com/answers/how-t

o-deal-with-tailgaters/

- *How to Overcome Fear on the Highway* https://getdriversed.com/blog-deta ils/overcome-fear-highway
- *How to Overcome Parking Anxiety* https://www.parkhound.com.au/blog/ho w-to-overcome-parking-anxiety/
- *Tag: signs of stress in drivers* https://www.gofleet.com/tag/signs-of-stress -in-drivers/
- *Gamification: a Novel Approach to Mental Health Promotion* https://pmc.nc bi.nlm.nih.gov/articles/PMC10654169/
- *Driving Anxiety Almost Ruined My Life—Here's How I ...* https://www.ahealt hypush.com/post/driving-anxiety-is-ruining-my-life
- *The 5 best habit tracker apps in 2025* https://zapier.com/blog/best-habit-tr acker-app/
- *How to Talk About Mental Health with Friends and Family* https://www.gran drisingbehavioralhealth.com/blog/how-to-talk-about-mental-health- with-friends-and-family
- *Tips on How to Overcome Fear of Driving* https://findmytherapist.com/reso urces/anxiety-stress/how-to-overcome-fear-of-driving/
- *Overcoming the Fear of Driving* https://adaa.org/webinar/consumer/overc oming-fear-driving
- *Driving and Anxiety - ADED* https://www.aded.net/page/Driving-Anxiety
- *Driving Anxiety is Ruining My Life: Tips to Regain Control* https://unconvent ionalpsychotherapy.com/driving-anxiety-is-ruining-my-life-tips-to-r egain-control/
- *A Driver's Guide on How to Get Over Driving Anxiety* https://www.gervelisla w.com/blog/how-to-get-over-driving-anxiety/
- *How to deal with change and uncertainty - Every Mind ...* https://www.nhs.u k/every-mind-matters/mental-wellbeing-tips/how-to-deal-with-chan ge/
- *Driving Anxiety is Ruining My Life: Tips to Regain Control* https://unconvent ionalpsychotherapy.com/driving-anxiety-is-ruining-my-life-tips-to-r egain-control/

www.ingramcontent.com/pod-product-compliance
Lightning Source LLC
Chambersburg PA
CBHW071531120626
46550CB00006B/2413